ECUADOR

FRAGILE
DEMOCRACY

David Corkill and David Cubitt

First published in Great Britain in 1988 by Latin America Bureau
(Research and Action) 1 Amwell Street, London EC1R 1UL

British Library Cataloguing in Publication Data

Corkill, David
    Ecuador: fragile democracy.
    1. Ecuador, to 1987
    I. Title   II. Cubitt, David
    986.6

    ISBN 0-906156-40-8
    ISBN 0-906156-39-4 Pbk

Written by David Corkill and David Cubitt
with additional material by Richard Hartill, Brenda Lipson, David Jackson,
Cover design by Chris Hudson
Photo by Marco Sandoval, *El Comercio*
Map by Michael Green © LAB
Typeset, printed and bound by Russell Press, Nottingham
Trade distribution in UK by TWP, 151 Stratford Road,
Birmingham B11 1RD
Distribution in the USA by Monthly Review Foundation

Contents

Ecuador in Brief

Country and People

Land area	275,341 sq.km.
Coastal region	25.0%
Highland region	26.2%
Amazon region	45.8%
Galápagos Islands	3.0%

Highest mountains	
Mt Chimborazo	6,267m
Mt Colopaxi	5,897m

Population (1986)	9,647,107
Annual growth rate (1986)	3.1%
Percentage in cities over 500,000 (1986)	51%
Quito	1,500,000
Guayaquil	2,200,000

The People

Mestizos (mixed Spanish and Indian)	40%
Amerindians	40%
Whites	15%
Blacks	5%

Main Indian groups	
Coastal	Cayapa
Highland	Quichua (over 2 million)
	Shuar (over 20,000)
Amazon tribes	Huaorani, Siona, Secoya, Cofan, Quichua, Shuar, Achuar (over 70,000)

Language	Spanish Quechua Other Amerindian languages
Religion	Roman Catholic (official and majority religion) Protestant/Evangelical (following recent missionary work) Amerindian religions
Literacy (1985)	85% males 80% females

Health

Infant mortality (per 1,000 births)	124 (1960) 67 (1985)
Life expectancy at birth	56 (1965) 65 (1985)
Malnutrition	67% (under fives) 18% (nursing/expectant mothers)

Housing (1982)

Urban	Rural
	41.9% (non-permanent)
89.3%	84.5% (no piped water)
85.7%	94.5% (no sewage)

Education

47.5% drop out of primary school
53.1% of those who reach secondary school drop out

The Economy

Total GDP	US$10,840 million
per capita GDP (1986)	US$1,124
per capita GDP (1987 post-earthquake estimate)	US$1,045

GDP growth rate — average annual growth rate (1965-84) 3.8%

1982	1.2
1983	-2.8
1984	4.0
1985	3.8
1986	1.7

vi

Income distribution
percentage of population below UNESCO absolute poverty level
(1974-84)   urban   40%
                             rural   65%

Inflation
Average annual rate   1965-73   6.2%
                             1973-84   17.8%
                             1987   35%

Employment
Percentage of working-age population in work — 43%*

	1965	1980
Agriculture	55	39
Industry	19	20
Services	26	42

*Excludes 'black economy' and subsistence non-marketed agriculture.

Trade

	Exports	US $ million		Imports
		oil %	non oil %	
1980	2,544	—	—	2,362
1981	2,324	68	32	2,220
1982	2,207	65	35	2,055
1983	2,365	74	26	1,408
1984	2,622	70	30	1,567
1985	2,905	66	34	1,611
1986	2,181	45	55	1,677

Other exports in order of economic importance: coffee, sea-food,
bananas, cocoa, fruit and vegetables (since 1986).

Ecuador suffered a double blow when the oil price collapsed: it obtained
less for its exports, yet the price of imported oil-based derivatives did not
fall by as much.

Recipients of oil exports
South Korea	41%
United States	29%
China	13%
Panama	8.5%
Brazil	8.5%

State spending (1983)
Public spending as a percentage of GDP — 14%
Defence   10%
Education   23%
Health   7.5%
Social Security   1.3%
Economic Services   13.9%
Other   40%

Sources: CEPAL; Collins World Atlas; International Bank for
Reconstruction and Development; International Development Bank,
National Bank of Ecuador; UNICEF.

Geographical Note

Ecuador, population 10,000,000 (approx.), lies on the Pacific coast of Latin America and is crossed by the equator from which it derives its name. The country (275,341 sq.km.) is one of the smaller South American republics and compares in area with the United Kingdom (244,102sq.km.).

The country is divided into three distinct geographical regions.

1. A coastal region of plains and low-lying hills mainly populated by *mestizos* and coastal indigenous Indians, apart from the department of Esmeraldas where blacks make up 50 per cent of the inhabitants. Just over half the population lives in the coastal region, over two million in the city of Guayaquil. Agriculture is export-oriented: cattle, bananas, African palm, rice, sugar, and coffee on the higher slopes.

2. The Andean *sierra* which forms part of the Andes mountain chain running along the Pacific side of the continent. In Ecuador this is composed of two main ridges running parallel from north to south. Volcanoes and mountains rise to heights of up to 6,267m. 46 per cent of Ecuador's population live in the *sierra*, mainly in the deep mountain valleys. Half the population of the *sierra* are Quichua Amerindians, while other indigenous groups and *mestizos* make up the rest. Quito, the capital city (pop. 1,500,000) is in this region. In contrast with the coast, most agricultural activity in the highlands is aimed at domestic consumption: animal-grazing, potatoes, maize and other cereals.

3. Further to the east lies Ecuador's Amazon territory. A further 174,565ksq.km. of Amazon land, currently administered by Peru, is also claimed by Ecuador. Until recently the area was largely uncultivated. Oil drilling began in 1967 and by the early 1980s large areas had been prepared for African palm cultivation. The region consists of extensive tropical rain forest, intersected by Amazon tributaries flowing eastwards from the Andes. The area is sparsely populated with Indian tribes and *mestizos* who have arrived in the wake of the oil and palm development. This development has destroyed large tracts of rain forest and is dramatically changing the ecosystem to the detriment of the Amerindians who depend on it for both hunting and gathering, and shifting cultivation.

ix

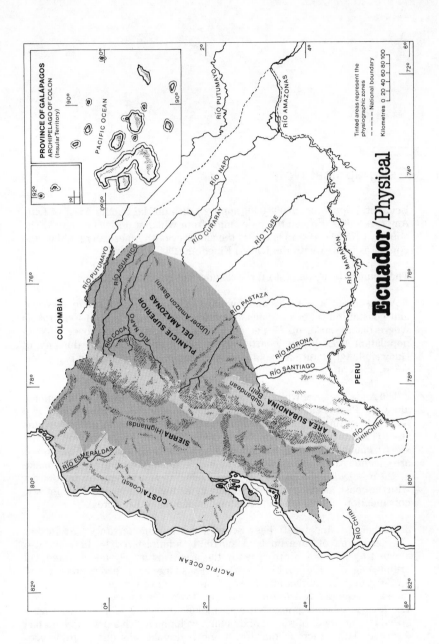

Ecuador/Physical

PROVINCE OF GALAPAGOS
ARCHIPELAGO OF COLON
(Insular Territory)

PACIFIC OCEAN

Tinted areas represent the
physiographic zones
– – – National boundary
Kilometres 0 20 40 60 80 100

COLOMBIA

PERU

PACIFIC OCEAN

RÍO PUTUMAYO

RÍO PUTUMAYO

RÍO AGUARICO

RÍO COCA

RÍO NAPO

RÍO NAPO

RÍO CURARAY

RÍO PASTAZA

RÍO TIGRE

RÍO AMAZONAS

RÍO MARAÑON

RÍO MORONA

RÍO SANTIAGO

RÍO CHINCHIPE

RÍO CHIRA

RÍO ESMERALDAS

PLANICIE SUPERIOR
DEL AMAZONAS
(Upper Amazon Basin)

SIERRA (Highlands)

ÁREA SUBANDINA (Subandean Belt)

COSTA (Coast)

x

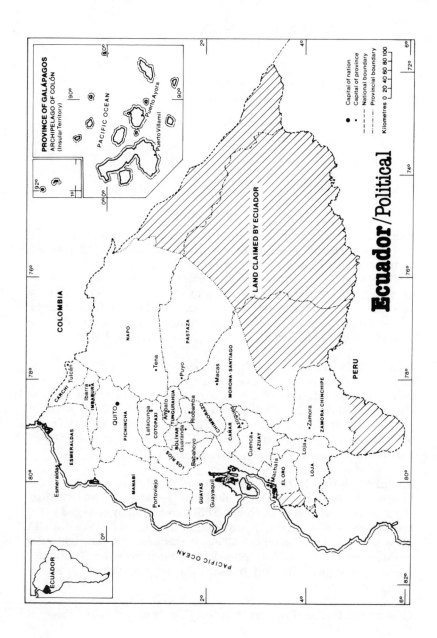

Ecuador/Political

LAND CLAIMED BY ECUADOR

PROVINCE OF GALÁPAGOS
ARCHIPELAGO OF COLÓN
(Insular Territory)

PACIFIC OCEAN

Puerto Ayora
Puerto Villamil

COLOMBIA

PERU

PACIFIC OCEAN

ECUADOR

Capital of nation
Capital of province
National boundary
Provincial boundary
Kilometres 0 20 40 60 80 100

CARCHI
Tulcán
IMBABURA
Ibarra
ESMERALDAS
Esmeraldas
PICHINCHA
QUITO
NAPO
Tena
COTOPAXI
Latacunga
Ambato
TUNGURAHUA
PASTAZA
Puyo
BOLÍVAR
Guaranda
CHIMBORAZO
Riobamba
LOS RÍOS
Babahoyo
MANABÍ
Portoviejo
GUAYAS
Guayaquil
MORONA·SANTIAGO
Macas
CAÑAR
Azogues
AZUAY
Cuenca
Loja
LOJA
ZAMORA·CHINCHIPE
Zamora
EL ORO
Machala

Political Parties

Radical Liberal Party *(Partido Liberal Radical,* PLR)
The PLR is all that remains of the traditional Liberal Party which dominated Ecuadorean politics from the late 19th century until the 1940s. Founded in 1878 to represent coastal business and commercial interests, it went into decline and split into various factions in the 1950s. In 1978 the PLR presidential candidate, Raúl Clemente Huerta, won third place in the first round of voting. Febres Cordero chose a Liberal, Blasco Peñaherrera, as his Vice-President in 1984.

Conservative Party *(Partido Conservador,* PC)
Ecuador's oldest political party, founded in 1855, the PC traditionally represents the interests of the *sierra* (highlands) oligarchy and the Catholic Church. Its decline was precipitated when younger, progressive elements left the party. The PC participated in the right-wing coalitions of 1978 and 1984 and took a seat in the Febres cabinet, but returned only one deputy to Congress in 1986.

Social Christian Party *(Partido Social Cristiano,* PSC)
Founded in the 1950s when Camilo Ponce Enriquez (President 1956-60) split from the Conservatives, the PSC has gradually emerged as the leading party of the Right. It was one of the main channels for CIA penetration in Ecuador in the 1960s. It has provided the right-wing coalition candidates in both presidential elections since democracy was restored in 1979, and became the second largest group in Congress in the 1986 elections.

Concentration of Popular Forces *(Concentración de Fuerzas Populares* CFP)
Founded in 1946 as a vehicle for the political ambitions of Carlos Guevara Moreno and later taken over by Asaad Bucaram, this populist

and ideologically incoherent party whose main base has been among the urban proletariat of the coast formed a coalition with the centre-left DP in 1978 to elect one of its members, Jaime Roldós Aguilera, to the presidency. The party immediately divided into two warring factions and its political fortunes have dipped dramatically ever since. From its position in 1979 as the largest party in Congress with 29 seats, the CFP was reduced to a rump of four deputies seven years later.

People, Change and Democracy *(Pueblo, Cambio y Democracia, PCD)*
The PCD, which was formed in 1980 by Jaime Roldós from among CFP defectors, was led by the late President's brother, León Roldós, until his resignation in early 1986. The PCD's subsequent shift to the centre-right was reflected in the acceptance by its new leader, Aquiles Rigail, of the post of Social Welfare Minister in the Febres cabinet.

Popular Democracy *(Democracia Popular, DP)*
This Christian Democratic party was first founded in 1964 and entered the government six years later. The party's base is in the *sierra* where it draws support from a middle class and rural constituency. A reformist party with a clearly-defined ideology and a technocratic image, it also has a following among employees in the state sector. In 1977 the DP formed a coalition with Julio César Trujillo's Progressive Conservatives, but allied itself with the CFP when the Electoral Tribunal banned its participation in the 1978 elections. The DP leader, Osvaldo Hurtado, was elected Vice-President in 1979 and on Roldós' death in an air crash, became President 1981-84. He is also President of the Christian Democratic Association of Latin America.

Democratic Left *(Izquierda Democrática, ID)*
Founded in the early 1970s when Rodrigo Borja split from the Liberals, ID is a social democratic party affiliated to the Socialist International and drawing its support from among the Quito middle class, the *sierra* peasantry, trade unionists and its network of *barrio* (neighbourhood) committees in many *sierra* towns. Since 1978 this modern, well-organised party progressed to become the largest single party in the last two congressional elections. After finishing in fourth place in the 1978 presidential contest, Borja stood again in 1984 when, after leading in the first round, he was narrowly defeated in the run-off by Febres Cordero. As the main opposition party, ID has suffered defections from among its 24 deputies and lost ground in 1986, but still remains the largest party in Congress.

Alfarist Radical Front *(Frente Radical Alfarista,* FRA)
Founded in 1972 by Abdón Calderón Muñoz, the populist and centre-right FRA draws most of its support from the peasantry in the coastal provinces of Guayas and El Oro. Its leader took fifth place in the first round of the 1978 presidential elections, but was assassinated soon afterwards. His daughter Cecilia Calderón de Castro succeeded him in the leadership, and benefiting from a sympathy vote, the FRA won 20 per cent of the vote in the 1980 municipal elections. In 1985 the FRA's five deputies joined the pro-government coalition, the FNR, and Iván Castro was elected Vice-President of the Congress.

Democratic Party *(Partido Demócrata,* PD)
Set up by former Liberal Francisco Huerta Montalvo, as a personal vehicle in the 1970s, the PD has a social democratic orientation and attracts middle-class support. In 1981 Huerta became Health Minister in the Roldós government. After increasing its representation to five seats in 1984, the PD suffered an internal split which resulted in three deputies joining the opposition FDP and the remaining two joining the FRN.

Popular Democratic Movement *(Movimiento Popular Democrático,* MPD)
Formed in the last years of the 1970s as a legal front of the pro-Albanian *Partido Comunista Marxista-Leninista de Ecuador* (PCMLE). With a political base in Esmeraldas and the southern province of Loja and support from inside the universities and the Teachers' Union, which it controls, the MPD has become one of the strongest parties on the Left. Under the leadership of Jaime González Hurtado, this sectarian group refused to join the broad left coalition FADI because of its antipathy to the PCE, but did cooperate with the anti-Febres opposition bloc after 1984 and increased its representation to four deputies in the 1986 elections. It has allied with FADI and other left groups to form the *Frente de Izquierda Unida* (FIU) for the 1988 elections.

Ecuadorean Socialist Party *(Partido Socialista Ecuatoriano,* PSE)
Originally founded in 1926, the Socialists, like other such parties in Latin America at the time, suffered a schism after the Cuban Revolution and divided into the *Partido Socialista Revolucionario Ecuatoriano* (PSRE) and the PSE. They draw support from among intellectuals, peasants and workers affiliated to both the CEDOC and CEOSL trade union federations. Longstanding divisions exist between

xiv

the social democrats and the left-wing led by Jorge Chiriboga, who took his faction into alliance with the PCE in 1978 as part of the FADI. It has entered an alliance with APRE to form the *Unión Patriótica del Pueblo* (UPP) for the 1988 elections.

Ecuadorean Roldocist Party *(Partido Roldocista Ecuatoriano, PRE)*
Set up in competition with the PCD by colleagues of Jaime Roldós who claimed to be the true heirs of the late President's political tradition, the PRE is part of the far-flung political network of the Bucaram clan. Under the leadership of Abdalá Bucaram Ortiz, Roldós' brother-in-law, the PRE, which derives its support from Guayaquil, gained five seats in Congress in 1986. Bucaram is the party's contender for the 1988 elections.

Ecuadorean Revolutionary Popular Action *(Acción Popular Revolucionaria Ecuatoriana, APRE)*
A minor party formed by Carlos Guevara Moreno in 1956 after he split from the CFP. It has largely been used as a personal political vehicle by various ambitious Guayaquil-based politicians, but has recently undergone a renaissance following reorganisation. It now attracts support from trade unionists and *barrio* dwellers in some of the major cities. In May 1987 APRE recruited General Vargas to its ranks and also incorporated part of the *Comité del Pueblo* which counts the well-known writer Jaime Galarza among its adherents. Vargas has become a candidate for the 1988 presidential elections with the backing of APRE, PSE and a faction from FADI.

Other political groupings

There are a number of political parties and movements which do not have legal recognition, but most participate in the elections in alliance with a legal front. The most significant are:

Communist Party of Ecuador *(Partido Comunista del Ecuador, PCE)*
Founded in 1931 in a split from the Socialist Party, it is pro-Soviet and termed as moderate Marxist with elections as a central part of its strategy, and open to developing alliances with some of the 'progressive' national bourgeois elements. It is the controlling influence in the CTE union central, and its base is drawn mainly from the middle classes and urban workers, with little peasant or student support. It publishes a weekly, *El Pueblo*. Internal divisions in 1987 led

to one faction participating with the UPP alliance in contradiction to the party's alliance with the FIU.

Marxist-Leninist Communist Party of Ecuador *(Partido Comunista Marxista-Leninista del Ecuador,* PCMLE)
Founded 1964, as a Maoist split from the PCE at the time of the Sino-Soviet split, it is now pro-Albanian. In 1977 it formed the MPD as its electoral front, and has been quite successful in broadening its support. The party controls the teachers union, and has formed the UGTE and *Frente Popular* and has recently appeared to overcome its sectarian tendencies to enter into greater coordination with other popular organisations and political parties. It publishes *En Marcha* weekly, and has a very hard working and efficient party machine. It participates in the FIU.

Revolutionary Socialist Party of Ecuador *(Partido Socialista Revolucionario del Ecuador,* PSRE)
Formed in a radical split from the Socialist Party in 1963, with no particular international alignment, it decided on a policy of 'entryism' into the Socialist Party and has successfully taken over the majority control and leadership. It has support from some of the student sector, urban workers, some of the peasant organisations and intellectuals, being strongest in Quito and Azuay. The party produces a monthly called *La Tierra.* It participates in the UPP.

Popular Socialist Party *(Partido Socialista Popular,* PSP)
A split from the PSRE, the PSP has close links with Cuba and is committed to an alliance with the PCE within FADI. It has influence within CEDOC and draws its support largely from the peasant and shanty-town sectors and young intellectuals. Recently it has become more radical since the change of leadership from Chiriboga. The party produces a monthly, *Venceremos* and participates in the FIU.

Revolutionary Workers Movement *(Movimiento Revolucionario de los Trabajadores,* MRT)
Founded 1977, since 1981 it has defined itself as revolutionary-Marxist and is affiliated to the Fourth International. It is strongest in Guayas and Canar, drawing its support largely from the peasant and shanty-town sectors, with some industrial workers and intellectuals. It participated in the 1986 elections with the Socialist Party, with one member returned as deputy for Canar. It now participates in the FIU. The party produces a monthly, *Lucha Socialista.*

Left Revolutionary Movement *(Movimiento de Izquierda Revolucionaria*, MIR)*
There are about seven MIR groupings, varying in size and influence. The strongest, led by Icaza, has its base in Quito among industrial workers, shanty-town dwellers and students. Most of the groupings are participating in the FIU.

Trade Unions

Ecuador has one of the smallest and, until recently, least influential trade union movements in Latin America. The majority of industrial and agricultural workers remain unorganised. Estimates of trade union membership are notoriously unreliable, but the level of unionisation has probably never exceeded 20 per cent of the workforce. While something like half of them belong to the three main national federations, the rest belong to small, independent, occupational, factory-based unions and artisan associations.

Workers United Front (*Frente Unitario de Trabajadores*, FUT)
FUT comprises the three main federations and a number of affiliated independent unions, and claims more than 300,000 members. Its leadership rotates among the leaders of the CEDOC, the CEOSL and the CTE. Since the economic crisis of the 1980s the FUT has, with varying degrees of of success, tried to establish itself as the focus for popular mass protest. The effectiveness of the FUT's strike calls has been compromised by ideological and political divisions and a tendency to press the wage demands of its more militant working class membership to the detriment of the demands of other sectors.

Ecuadorean Confederation of Free Trade Union Organisations
(*Confederación Ecuatoriana de Organizaciones Sindicales Libres*, CEOSL)
CEOSL was originally founded by the pro-US *Organización Regional Interamericana del Trabajo* (ORIT) in 1962, but adopted a socialist and social democratic orientation during the 1970s. It has become the largest of the confederations by combining a strong industrial base alongside recruits from the growing service sector and some agricultural and peasant workers, principally on the sugar plantations. Its leader is José Chávez.

xviii

Confederation of Ecuadorean Workers *(Confederación de Trabajadores del Ecuador, CTE)*
The CTE was founded in 1944 and is linked to the pro-Moscow Communist Party and affiliated to the World Federation of Trade Unions (WFTU). Traditionally the most militant confederation, the CTE has declined from its peak in the 1960s and its peasant wing, the *Federación Ecuatoriana de Indios* (FEI) is no longer the force that it once was. The CTE is headed by the electricity workers' leader, Edgar Ponce, and draws support mainly from industrial and public sector workers, artisans and autonomous workers such as street-vendors.

Ecuadorean Confederation of Class Organisations *(Confederación Ecuatoriana de Organizaciones Clasistas, CEDOC)*
Originally Catholic in inspiration and closely linked to Christian Democracy, the confederation split in 1976 when the Marxist leadership withdrew from the *Central Latinoamericano de Trabajadores* (CLAT). CEDOC-Socialista took the bulk of the membership into a closer alliance with the FUT and CTE. The old leadership retained the CEDOC name and is still affiliated to CLAT. Eighty per cent of CEDOC-S members are peasants who belong to the *Federación Nacional de Organizaciones Campesinas* (FENOC), the largest peasant union in Ecuador, under the leadership of Mesias Tatamuez.

Independent Unions

There is a large number of independent occupational and artesanal unions which are not affiliated to the FUT. They include FETRACEPE (state sector petroleum workers) and CONASEP (public sector employees). The militant teachers' union, *Unión General de Trabajadores del Ecuador* (UGTE), a PCML-led rival to the FUT which also mobilises the student unions. The peasant union ECUARUNARI was founded in 1971 under left-wing Christian auspices with the aim of providing the indigenous population with its own organisation. It now forms part of the *Confederación de Nacionalidades Indígenas del Ecuador* (CONAIE), which represents all Indian organisations and nations from the coast, *sierra* (highlands), and *oriente* (eastern region).

Plebiscites and Elections in Ecuador 1978-86

Constitutional Referendum
(January 1978)

New Constitution	778,611 (43%)
1945 Constitution	582,556 (32%)
Spoiled Ballots	421,510 (23%)

Presidential Elections
(Second Round)

April 1979		May 1984	
Jaime Roldós (CFP-DP)	68.5%	León Febres Cordero (FRN)	51.5%
Sixto Durán (FNC)	31.5%	Rodrigo Borja (ID)	48.5%

Congressional Elections

Party	April 1979 (69 seats)	January 1984 (71 seats)	June 1986 (71 seats)
Izquierda Democrática (ID)	15	24	17
Democracia Popular (DP)	—	4	8
Partido Roldocista Ecuatoriano (PRE)	—	3	5
Movimiento Popular Democrático (MPD)	1	3	4
Frente Amplio de Izquierda	—	2	3
Partido Socialista (PSE)	—	1	6
Partido Social Cristiano (PSC)	3	9	15
Partido Demócrata (PD)	—	5	1
Concentración de Fuerzas Populares (CFP)	29	7	4
Frente Radical Alfarista(FRA)	—	6	3
Partido Liberal Radical (PLR)	4	4	3
Partido Conservador (PC)	10	2	1
Partido Nacional Revolucionario (PNR)	2	1	—
Partido Nacional Velasquista	1	—	—
Coalición Institucionalista Democrática	3	—	—
Pueblo, Cambio y Democracia (PCD)	—	—	1

Constitutional Plebiscite
(June 1986)

For Amendment	682,164 (30.4%)
Against Amendment	1,561,853 (69.6%)

Presidential Elections January 1988[1]
(Candidates and running mates)

		First round vote + % of valid vote	
1. Rodrigo Borja Luis Parodi	ID	505,574	24.1
2. Sixto Durán Pablo Baquerizo	PSC	318,990	15.2
3. Angel Duarte Teresa Minuche	CFP	154,979	7.4
4. Abdalá Bucaram Hugo Caicedo	PRE	368,900	17.6
5. Frank Vargas Enrique Ayala	APRE	280,562	13.4
6. Jamil Mahaud Juan José Pons	DP	243,002	11.6
7. Jaime Hurtado Ernesto Alvarez	MPD FADI	97,767	4.6
8. Carlos Julio Emanuel Pedro José Arteta	FRA	66,888	3.2
9. Miguel Albornez Roberto Goldblum	PL	29,326	1.4
10. Guillermo Sotomayor	PR[2]	23,974	1.1

1. Provisional results based on figures from *El Comercio* 2.2.1988.
2. Newly formed Republican Party.

List of Abbreviations

APRE	Acción Popular Revolucionaria Ecuatoriana Ecuadorean Revolutionary Popular Action
AVC	Alfaro Vive, Carajo Alfaro lives, OK
BDP	Bloque Democrático Progresista Progressive Democratic Bloc
CEDOC	Confederación Ecuatoriana de Organizaciones Clasistas Ecuadorean Confederation of Class Organisations
CEOSL	Confederación Ecuatoriana de Organizaciones Sindicales Libres Ecuadorean Confederation of Free Trade Union Organisations
CFP	Concentración de Fuerzas Populares Concentration of Popular Forces
CID	Coalición Institucionalista Democrática Institutional Democratic Coalition
CLAT	Central Latinoamericana de Trabajadores Latin American Workers Confederation
CTE	Confederación de Trabajadores del Ecuador Confederation of Ecuadorean Workers
DP	Democracia Popular Popular Democracy
CONAIE	Confederación de Nacionalidades Indígenas del Ecuador Ecuadorean Confederation of Indigenous Peoples
CONFENIAE	Confederación de Nacionalidades Indígenas de la Amazonia Ecuatoriana

	Confederation of Indigenous Peoples of the Ecuadorean Amazon
ECUARUNARI	Ecuador Runacunapac Riccharimui
FADI	Frente Amplio de la Izquierda Broad Left Front
FEI	Federación Ecuatoriana de Indios Ecuadorean Indian Federation
FENOC	Federación Nacional de Organizaciones Campesinas National Federation of Peasant Organisations
FIU	Frente de Izquierda Unidaq United Left Front
FRA	Frente Radical Alfarista Alfarist Radical Front
FRN	Frente de Reconstrucción Nacional Front for National Reconstruction
FUT	Frente Unitario de Trabajadores Workers United Front
ID	Izquierda Democrática Democratic Left
IERAC	Instituto Ecuatoriano de Reforma Agraria y Colonización Agrarian Reform Institute
IMF	International Monetary Fund
MIR	Movimiento de Izquierda Revolucionaria Left Revolutionary Movement
MPD	Movimiento Popular Democrático Popular Democratic Movement
MRT	Movimiento Revolucionario de los Trabajadores Revolutionary Workers Movement
OPEC	Organisation of Petroleum Exporting Countries
PC	Partido Conservador Conservative Party
PCD	Pueblo, Cambio y Democracia People, Change and Democracy
PCE	Partido Comunista Ecuatoriano Communist Party of Ecuador
PCMLE	Partido Comunista Marxista-Leninista de Ecuador Marxist-Leninist Communist Party of Ecuador
PD	Partido Demócrata Democratic Party
PLR	Partido Liberal Radical Radical Labour Party

Introduction

Ecuador is not a 'notorious' Latin American country in the way that others are or have been. Though it has had military governments, it has never been a byword for military despotism and the gross and persistent abuse of human rights which has characterised countries like Argentina, Brazil or Chile at various times. Though it has had many revolutions, none has been as hugely violent and deep-seated as Mexico's or as radical and far-reaching as Cuba's. Though it has a substantial Amerindian population and once formed part of the Inca empire, the place of the Amerindians in national society has not been subject to intense debate in the way that it has been in Mexico or Peru. Though it has been the victim of external aggression by its Latin American neighbours and economic penetration by the United States, it had not been reduced to the condition of extreme dependence which has characterised the Central American and Caribbean republics for much of the 20th century. Though it has had, and has, a tradition of violent political dissent and active guerrilla movements, these have not been as widespread and threatening to the status quo as the guerrilla movements in Colombia or Bolivia. Although it was at one time – literally – a 'banana republic', it has also experienced a measure of development and therefore has some of the characteristics of other relatively developed Latin American countries. Ecuador seldom makes the headlines in the world's press.

The same reasons that make Ecuador not a 'notorious' country, however, also make it especially worth examining as a Latin American one. In some ways it is the most purely 'typical' Latin American republic. On many indices or statistics for the region, from area and population to racial composition, from class structure to levels of development, Ecuador tends time after time to emerge as the median case where we can find something of every other country. Looking at Ecuador, in other words, can tell us a lot about Latin America as a whole.

1

Ecuador is important on its own terms, too. It provides an interesting case study, from which lessons can be learned, of a poor developing country which suddenly and fortuitously finds itself endowed with unprecedented riches in the form of vast oil reserves. The oil boom which began in the early 1970s seemed at first to hold out the promise of escape from poverty, underdevelopment and dependence, a chance to build a dynamic and developed economy based on greater social justice. In fact, it became clear as the oil boom progressed that, while some sectors of the population were becoming relatively prosperous and even wealthy, the more ambitious expectations had been frustrated.

The country's socio-economic structures and political culture have proved to be stubbornly resilient and have created as great a constraint on development as have the earlier lack of natural resources or the inadequacy of investment finance. Since 1972 three quite distinct kinds of government – one a military dictatorship, two elected constitutional regimes – have wrestled with the problems of Ecuador. The military government of Rodríguez Lara pursued a state-directed 'developmentalist' policy modelled on the experience of the Peruvian military a few years earlier. The return of democracy in 1979 brought the social democrat and reformist policies of Jaime Roldós and Osvaldo Hurtado. This was followed by the all-out free-market policies of Febres Cordero, which briefly made Ecuador the darling of the international banking community. None of these three quite different regimes and quite different approaches has had more than limited success in overcoming Ecuador's problems and setting it unequivocally on the road to economic growth and social wellbeing.

This is not just a case of another military government mishandling and dissipating an unprecedented bonanza. Both military and civilian elites have failed to meet popular expectations during the 1970s and 1980s. While the military squandered oil revenues on expensive weaponry and ran up a huge foreign debt which later became an albatross around the nation's neck, the civilian administrations after 1979 turned out to be little better as custodians and managers of Ecuador's resources, allowing an obsession with political manoeuvring and constitutional issues to distract them from the more urgent tasks facing them. The balance-sheet for Ecuador since 1972, when we examine it from the perspective of the late 1980s, does not give many grounds for optimism about the country's immediate future either in political or economic terms.

Part of the reason why the entrenched socio-economic structures and political culture have been able to deflect the promise of oil-based development can be found in the evolution of a system of relationships

2

that rests on, and integrates, social status, economic predominance, regional loyalties and racial character. In the course of the book, we have tried to sketch out the main features of this system of relationships, showing how and why some are able to make it work to their benefit, while others, the forgotten majority, are excluded from it. The socio-economic system underpins the political system, and has given rise to the distinctive European style of Ecuadorean politics, an important feature of which is populism. Populist politics rest on the personality of particular leaders rather than their programmes, on contempt for conventional democratic practices as unable to express the 'real will' of the people, on vague appeals to nationalist sentiment and popular radicalism, on hostility to the ideology of class struggle and organised political parties. In Ecuador its master practitioner was José María Velasco Ibarra, who for nearly four decades, whether in or out of office, was at the centre of the country's political life. Although Velasco Ibarra died in 1979 and the political movement he left behind him no longer counts as a significant force, the style and techniques of political action that were developed in his heyday still shape, for good or ill, many of the ways in which political life is carried on. Whether Ecuador will succeed in overcoming the worst defects of its populist inheritance, and consolidate a genuine and functioning democracy, is still an open question.

1. From Incas to Oil

Long before the arrival of the Spanish *conquistadores* in the 16th century, the indigenous Indians of Ecuador had developed advanced cultures and a high level of civilisation, of which the Incas were only the latest and most sophisticated representatives. Pottery and ceramics, elaborate and beautiful textiles, the working of precious metals, complex irrigation systems, long-distance roads and a state postal service were all known. The well-organised agricultural base, supported by fishing and pastoral activities, was capable of supporting a large population, around half a million on the eve of the conquest. Society and political institutions, in the form of a religious-military despotism, were highly developed. Oceanic voyaging was known, and some historians think that there were contacts between Ecuador and Polynesia, or even Japan and China in pre-Columbian times.

The tribes of the *sierra*, the highlands around Quito, were warlike people – when Francisco Pizarro seized the Inca ruler Atahualpa in 1532 and began the Spanish conquest of Peru, the *conquistadores* found that some of the fiercest and most vigorous resistance came from the Ecuadorean Indians of the Inca professional army. They formed the backbone of the defence of the Inca capital Cuzco in 1533 and faced the Spanish on many other occasions in central Peru. After the execution of Atahualpa by Pizarro and the ending of effective resistance in Peru, the leading Inca General, Rumiñavi, withdrew with the Quito contingents to Ecuador to continue the fight.

Colonial Ecuador

The Spanish conquest of Ecuador began in earnest in 1534 when two rival bands, that of Pedro de Alvarado from the coast and Sebastián de Benalcázar's through the mountains, converged on Quito. At Teocajas,

5

north of modern Cuenca, the greatest pitched battle of the conquest was fought in May 1534, and in the last stages of the Spanish invasion, from Riobamba to Quito itself, fighting was almost continuous. When they did finally break into the city in June, the Spanish found that Rumiñavi had burned it and withdrawn with all the treasure and that many of the inhabitants had fled. It was refounded as the Spanish city of San Francisco de Quito on 28 August 1534. Warfare continued until near the end of the year, when Rumiñavi was captured and executed by the Spanish in the main square of the new capital. Like Cuauhtémoc in Mexico, Rumiñavi was the last great defender of the pre-Columbian world against the onslaught of European civilisation and deserves a special place in Ecuadorean history. With his death, organised Inca resistance came to an end. The savagery of the *conquistadores* during this campaign – torture, hangings, burning alive, throwing to the dogs, the sacking of whole towns and villages were commonly resorted to – was answered by the defenders' atrocities against those Indians who had joined the Spanish invaders. Both sides freely requisitioned foodstuffs and livestock, conscripted men, women and children as porters and burned and destroyed the countryside. By the end of the conquest, parts of Ecuador were a desolate ruin which took years to recover. The Indian population fell by around 60 per cent (from approximately half a million to less than a quarter of a million) by the end of the 16th century as a result of starvation, forced labour, and the diseases brought by the Europeans.

With the *conquistadores* came the churchmen. Monasteries were founded in the main towns in the 1530s and 1540s, though missionary work was delayed by civil wars between the Spanish and by a shortage of suitable priests. The first bishop of Quito arrived in 1549. Another early arrival was the Franciscan friar Jodoco Ricke, celebrated for importing the first wheat seeds and teaching European agricultural techniques to the natives of Quito. Such protection as the Indians received in the early years of the colony from the depredations of the *conquistadores* was given by the few missionaries who seriously concerned themselves with their condition.

The colonial system very quickly took shape in Ecuador and remained almost unchanged for the next 300 years. A small elite of 'Spaniards' – either from Spain itself or born in America – controlled economic life and monopolised land and trade. Jobs in the bureaucracy, the army, the church and the town councils were restricted to this group. Socially, they distinguished themselves from the rest of the population by their European racial origins, their traditional Hispanic culture and language, and their orthodox and conservative Catholicism (at the end of the colonial period, the

6

2,000 year-old gold and platinum ornament from La Tolita, north-west coast. The earliest known use of platinum anywhere.

Liberator Simón Bolívar was to describe Ecuador as 'a monastery'). Concentrated in the towns, both for their own safety amidst a sea of non-whites and for the pleasures and conveniences of urban life, their imposing residences – large enough to accommodate retinues of servants, slaves and hangers-on besides their own immediate families – may still be seen in the towns of the Ecuadorean highlands. They set the values for the ruling class in a mould which persists, in many cases, into the present day.

Below the elite were the *mestizos* (mixed Spanish-Indian) who formed the majority of the population in the larger towns and predominated in skilled trades, artisan occupations, small-scale commerce and retailing, and services. They lived insecurely between the elite whose status they envied and aspired to share and the masses whose sullen resentment they feared. If they were lucky or smart, they sometimes succeeded in working their way up into the ruling class. If they were unlucky, they sank down into the anonymous poverty and indigence of the masses. Discontented and resentful, they were easily incited to riot, sedition and disorder, and later to political mobilisation. In a society where wealth for those not born to it was more easily obtained by luck (winning a lottery, say) or pulling off a sharp deal, rather than by hard work, they placed emphasis on *viveza* (being 'street-wise'). As far as the elite were concerned, they were the *chusma*, the urban rabble.

The overwhelming majority of the population – even after the ravages of the conquest – were the Indians. Most worked on the estates of the great landholders, to whom they were distributed as forced labour after the conquest and then held by elaborate mechanisms of debt peonage and legal servitude. Others laboured in conditions indistinguishable from slavery in the *obrajes*, primitive textile factories which flourished in the highlands (Quito was the main centre of *obraje* textile production in America), or as porters, servants and labourers in the towns. In the more inaccessible parts of the colony, some tribes succeeded in preserving their ancient ways of life and a measure of autonomy, though it was always under threat from the encroaching frontier of Spanish settlement. All Indians were liable to pay tributes, the main source of revenue for the colonial government, and were the only group in society to pay direct taxes. Tributes were not abolished until 1820 on the coast and 1857 in the highlands.

Finally, there was a black and mulatto (mixed Spanish-black) population. This was small by comparison with other parts of Spanish America (about 8,000 slaves and 42,000 free persons of colour at the end of the 18th century), but played a decisive role in the export-oriented sugar-cane and cocoa plantations of the hot and humid Pacific coast area, where, it was thought, highland Indians were unsuited to field labour. Black resistance to the status quo was widespread and usually took the form of flight to one of the many communities of escaped slaves which were formed in the rugged and inaccessible northwest of the country. Indeed, for more than half a century a virtually independent black kingdom flourished in Esmeraldas and to the present day this region is more African in its racial composition and culture than anywhere else in the country.

8

Independence to Dependence:
the 19th and early 20th Centuries

Ecuador was an active exporting economy from early colonial times, mostly of crude textiles for Peru and Colombia, and also of livestock products and some gold. But towards the end of the 18th century a new product emerged. This was cocoa, the 'golden bean', which dominated Ecuador's foreign trade throughout the 19th and early 20th centuries. The effect of the cocoa boom was to reinforce the economic and social power of the elite. It delayed the emancipation of the Indians and blacks who became more than ever necessary as servile labour in the expanding plantations, and dramatically shifted the centre of gravity of the Ecuadorean economy towards Guayaquil, the thriving port city through which virtually all of Ecuador's trade passed.

These economic and social realities determined the course of Ecuadorean independence. In 1809 a clique of creole aristocrats in Quito overthrew the Spanish administration and installed a governing junta under the presidency of one of their number, the Marquis of Selva Alegre. Their aims were to abolish Spanish trade monopolies, lower taxes, and occupy financially rewarding posts in the bureaucracy themselves. They showed little inclination to defend the interests of *mestizos*, Indians or slaves – indeed, their fear of these groups led them to negotiate a return to their obedience to the crown almost immediately. The royal viceroy in Peru had little difficulty in putting down this rebellion and a subsequent, marginally more popular one in 1810-12.

When the next movement for independence came in 1820, it started not in Quito but in Guayaquil, where the incipient landowning and commercial bourgeoisie were anxious to promote free trade and expand the cocoa industry. Even so, the revolutionaries were unable to free the colony on their own, but had to depend on outside help, first from San Martín, the liberator of Peru, and then from Simón Bolívar, the liberator of Colombia. The consequence of this was that, when the royalist army was finally defeated at the battle of Pichincha (24 May 1822: the battle took place just outside the city of Quito, but the inhabitants of the city made no move to assist in their liberation), the Ecuadorean provinces were forcibly incorporated into Bolívar's visionary new state of Gran Colombia. Here the Ecuadoreans remained until 1830, growing increasingly restive under a military government run by Venezuelans and Colombians ('The last day of despotism and the first day of the same' was an Ecuadorean quip that began to circulate soon after Pichincha), paying taxes which seemed only to swell the incomes of politicians in Bogotá, the capital, and forced to fight in 1828-29 in a brief war with Peru, their main trading partner. Finally, in May 1830, the Ecuadoreans broke free from Colombia and established an independent state; ominously, this movement was also led by a foreigner and a soldier, the ambitious Venezuelan general Juan José Flores, who in pursuit of his ambition was forced to pay the price of surrendering Ecuadorean territory in what is today southwestern Colombia. (see Appendix 1)

For the next 65 years Ecuador passed from one government to another at sometimes dizzying speed. Of the 21 individuals and juntas which occupied the presidency a total of 34 times between 1830 and 1895, only six completed their constitutional term of office. The most notorious of the 19th century *caudillos* (strongmen) – who dominated politics either openly from the president's chair or from behind the scenes through clients and puppet ministers – were Flores himself (President 1830-34 and 1839-45); José María Urbina (President 1851-58) who abolished slavery in 1851, but otherwise imposed a stern military despotism on the country; Gabriel García Moreno (President 1860-65 and 1869-75), a religious zealot who dedicated the republic to the Sacred Heart of Jesus and tried to impose universal Catholic orthodoxy on all citizens by force; and Ignacio Veintimilla (President 1876-83), who achieved the unique feat of uniting all factions in the country against his dictatorship. Although there were several presidents from the coast in this period, the common feature of most 19th century governments was that they represented the interests of the conservative landowning and bureaucratic elite of Quito and the highlands against the commercial mentality of the agro-exporting bourgeoisie, the *monos* (monkeys) as they disdainfully called them, of Guayaquil and the coast.

Beneath the apparent sterility of political life, changes never ceased to occur in the economic structures as Ecuador was integrated more and more into the international economy and opened up to new ideas and values. On the coast, a money economy emerged based on entrepreneurial capitalism and wage labour, even before black slavery was abolished. In contrast, in the highlands a subsistence economy and servile labour flourished into the 20th century, based on *concertaje* and, later, *huasipungo*, forms of debt servitude inherited from the colonial period. The first attempts to establish banks in Guayaquil date from the 1830s, though banking did not get permanently under way until 1860. From the 1860s increasing world demand for Ecuador's traditional and new export products – cocoa (up from 6,036,000 kilos in 1847 to 25,723,000 kilos in 1899), coffee (up

A sierra *family; the Ecuadorean highlands have historically been a relatively poor and isolated area given over to subsistence farming.*

from 14,000 kilos in 1847 to 1,769,000 kilos in 1899), and palm nuts (14,654,000 kilos in 1899) – led to big profits for the coastal producers and shippers, the bankers who financed their activities, and for growing government revenues. Much of the latter was spent on the military, but some went into social, educational, technical and construction activities as well.

In 1895 the anti-clerical and market-oriented interests of the coastal elites triumphed in the 'Liberal Revolution' led by Eloy Alfaro (President 1895-1901 and 1906-11), who had been a guerrilla fighter against García Moreno and Veintimilla, a successful businessman in exile in Panama, and a revolutionary soldier in the Cuban struggles for independence. The Liberals immediately began to implement an ambitious programme of reform and development which they expected would bring Ecuador rapidly into the modern world. This included the construction or extension of railways, ports and roads. The Liberals also attacked the power of the church, introduced secular education and civil marriage and divorce and confiscated church lands. Eloy Alfaro's government also brought about the abolition of capital punishment.

The Liberal programme worked as long as cocoa exports and prices were high, but the advent of the First World War (1914-18) initiated a

11

period of crisis in the cocoa market which had important political and economic repercussions. Rather than cut back on the public works to which they were committed, the Liberals preferred to borrow from the banks and increase the supply of money in circulation. This in turn led to inflation and unemployment; strikes were violently suppressed and a feeling of social crisis grew among the conservative *serranos* (highlanders), who blamed the 'corrupt coastal oligarchy' of Guayaquil bankers and Liberal politicians for the country's problems. In the 1925 'July Revolution' a group of young military officers overthrew the government and began what they believed would be a programme of national regeneration.

The 1925 'July Revolution'

Most of the young military men who staged the 'July Revolution' were probably motivated by pure careerism and dislike of the way that promotions were manipulated. Their complaint was that 'the old customs go on: the political soldier is enthroned above the trained officer ... Young men who've studied hard and made an honest beginning to their career find promotion almost impossible because the top military ranks are obtained only by those who can pull strings or are political adventurers or are wealthy and socially well-connected' (Cueva, 1982). Another numerous group wanted to restore the importance of the highlands in the balance of power. Their view reflected the fact that most officers in the army were recruited from the landowning class in the *sierra* and were becoming more and more middle-class and bureaucratic in their outlook. Some – a minority – were also motivated by the desire to sweep away both the coastal oligarchy of Guayaquil bankers and the 'feudal' highlands landlords, and replace them with a more dynamic industrial and entrepreneurial class, responsive to the needs of the urban and rural working classes.

By the 1920s the expanded educational sector created by the Liberals had produced an active group of intellectuals and professionals who were influenced by socialist ideas. They were disillusioned by the failure of the 1895 'revolution' to bring about real change and eliminate the economic power of the elite, and were committed to political involvement with working-class organisations and the peasant movements among the Indians. Some of them believed the army's coup d'etat would lead to a new and genuine reform – after all, the leaders of the coup started by announcing that their regime would see 'equality for all and the protection of the proletarian'. But they were quickly disillusioned as it became clear

12

that for most army officers, the interests of their profession came before other ideals. Their notions of socialism were nearer to Mussolini's than to Marx's, and their intention was to reorganise Ecuadorean capitalism by force if necessary. Their policies were very much on the lines favoured by the major foreign powers. The British ambassador had said in 1923 that 'the real solution of Ecuador would be a man of the stamp of Porfirio Díaz of Mexico to run the country with an iron hand, assisted by foreign and honest officials'.

The military-backed dictatorship of Isidro Ayora (President 1926-31) seemed for a moment to be just such a regime. With the assistance of the North American Kemmerer economic mission, it devalued the currency which helped exporters in the highlands at the cost of putting up consumer prices for the poor, founded the Central Bank of Ecuador and carried through some banking reforms. Some labour legislation was also passed, to regulate hours and conditions of work, which benefited the small group of organised workers in the urban textile and public service industries, but ignored the plight of the much larger numbers of rural workers and marginally employed or unemployed urban workers. Finally, the regime devoted much energy to 'public cleansing' and 'moral reform' (as one commentator pointed out, 'prohibitions on entering markets, public buildings, schools, parks and theatres without wearing shoes – but no reforms which gave the unshod means to buy them'). In reality, the 'July Revolution' was simply a political readjustment to bring the coastal commercial and banking elite into a new balance with highland landowning and bureaucratic elites, and to give a modest but assured place in the power structure to middle-class and military interests. It laid out the power relationships which dominated the next four and a half decades.

Instability and *Velasquismo*, 1931-48

The Ayora government came to an end as the direct result of an economic crisis brought on by the Great Crash of 1929 in the US. In common with other Latin American countries, Ecuador experienced a sharp decline in the quantity and the price of its main exports. Between 1928 and 1931, cocoa exports went down from 23,737,000 kilos to 13,839,000 kilos and the price fell by 58.8 per cent. Coffee exports went down from 9,150,000 kilos to 8,337,000 kilos and the price fell by 65.7 per cent. Palm nut exports went down from 23,826,000 kilos to 20,082,000 kilos and the price fell by 47.7 per cent. The total value of exports fell from 15 million dollars in 1928 to less

13

than 7 million in 1931. The collapse of exports and the paralysis of business alienated the commercial elite, the massive cuts in public expenditure (21.5 per cent between 1928 and 1931) offended the bureaucratic middle class, and the equally massive increase in unemployment provoked growing popular discontent, especially among the urban working class.

The early 1930s were marked by a succession of demonstrations and protests and even (in August 1932) a four-day 'civil war' in the capital. With the 'July Revolution' discredited, Ayora was overthrown in 1931 and another period of extreme political instability supervened. Between 1931 and 1948 Ecuador had 21 governments, none of which succeeded in completing its term of office. Meanwhile, although exports and the economy in general started to recover after 1935, the economic crisis unleashed a wave of inflation and spiralling consumer prices which continued throughout the 1930s and early 1940s. The value of the national currency, the *sucre*, fell by 65.2 per cent against the dollar between 1930 and 1943, and the cost of living rose by 298.3 per cent. The impoverished popular classes were threatened with actual starvation.

Against this background flourished José María Velasco Ibarra, undoubtedly the most extraordinary and – to his followers – captivating personality in modern Ecuadorean politics. (see Appendix 2) Five times President (1934-35, 1944-47, 1952-56, 1960-61, 1968-72) but only once completing his mandate, for a generation he was, whether in or out of office, the dominant piece on the political chessboard. Velasco Ibarra was in fact the creator and supreme practitioner of a new kind of politics in 20th century Ecuador, the politics of populism. *Velasquismo* – Ecuador's own brand of populism – was made up of three basic ingredients. First was *personalismo*. Velasco's carefully cultivated image of personal austerity, honesty and poverty combined with a vibrant and fiery oratory. His fierce denunciations of the misdeeds and immorality of the rich and privileged, and promises of quick solutions to national problems and better times ahead, made a powerful appeal to the popular masses. Second was street politics. *Velasquismo* raised to an art the techniques of orchestrated street action, marches and demonstrations, the control of the streets and even public buildings by 'popular multitudes', the intimidation of political opponents inside and outside Congress by gangs of rowdies, and the resort to violence. Third was the ideology. This included patriotic nationalism, replete with appeals to 'the Fatherland' and a strong nationalist stance in foreign affairs and hostility to party politics in favour of 'movements' which could integrate differing political tendencies. Velasco

14

persistently denounced political parties as divisive and unrepresentative of social and national reality and, though he was willing to accept their support whatever their political complexion, was never beholden to them. It also included belief in the need for 'strong leadership' and the virtues of dictatorship when ordinary constitutional forms did not meet the leader's needs. Finally, *Velasquismo* emphasised moral regeneration. Velasco's view was that Ecuador's problems were not due to social, economic or class conflict, but to lack of morality and civic responsibility.

Most of Velasco's electoral support came from the unorganised masses struggling to survive in the squalid conditions of the rapidly expanding cities. Between 1933 and 1974 the population of Pichincha province, capital Quito, rose from 261,902 to 981,053 and that of Guayas province, capital Guayaquil, from 351,438 to 1,512,838. With this popular force behind him, Velasco was able time after time to push his way into the presidency against the reluctance of the elites to accept him. When they did accept him, they did so warily and only because they saw him as the lesser of two evils, as the means by which the popular masses could be co-opted and prevented from falling into the lap of Marxist parties. Their willingness to tolerate him therefore lay within narrow boundaries. As long as his popular support was sufficient to intimidate and overawe them, as long as his speeches and actions were moralising and 'radical' but not ideological and 'left-wing',as long as he avoided the temptation to seize the dictatorship, they put up with him. When he frittered away his popular support, or seemed to go too far in the direction of genuine structural reform, or became cavalier about civil rights, they overthrew him.

The ephemeral governments of the 1931-48 period represented only the struggles between different factions of the landowning and commercial elites, the middle class and the military for control of the presidency and the Congress. The balance of power shifted marginally one way or the other between them, but little real change occurred. Velasco Ibarra made three attempts at the presidency in this period.

His first occupancy of the presidency came in 1934 against the background of a frontier dispute between Colombia and Peru. The government of Martínez Mera wanted to follow a policy of non-involvement, but Velasco argued for 'patriotic' intervention on the Colombian side against the 'historic enemy' Peru. Martínez Mera was forced out of office, largely as a result of Velasco's attacks on him, and in the subsequent election – one of the few fair ones – Velasco romped home with over 80 per cent of the vote. He had been forced on the elite by the unusual circumstances of the moment; their reluctance to accept him aroused his authoritarian instincts. He soon resorted to

15

censorship of the press, arrest of opponents and suspension of civil liberties. Finally, when he attempted to proclaim himself dictator, the army ejected him from the presidency and turned it back over to the elite.

In the election of 1940 the elite's candidate was Dr Carlos Arroyo del Río, who was linked to foreign importing companies. To ensure his election and keep out Velasco, with his rhetoric and his 'rabble', they resorted to electoral fraud on a massive scale:

'At 8.00pm on the 10th of January the newsreaders of the State radio station announced the electoral triumph of Velasco Ibarra; at 10.00pm they reported that the result had gone to Arroyo. Barely populated provinces like Manabí, occupied only by illiterates and ruled by rural bosses, produced fantastic numbers of votes, more than the number of citizens qualified to vote. Guayaquil, which Dr Arroyo couldn't even visit during the election campaign, so unanimously had he been rejected by the populace ... produced a large number of votes for him.' (Cueva, 1982)

Velasco's refusal to accept the result and his obvious preparations to stage a coup d'etat led to the imposition of martial law and his exile to Colombia.

By 1944 the correlations of power had changed again. The Arroyo del Río government was discredited by Ecuador's defeat in the 1941 war with Peru and the loss of her Amazon territories by the Río Protocol, and also by a popular uprising in Guayaquil in protest against government repression of workers' demonstrations. Arroyo fell from power and Velasco was recalled from exile to be the saviour of the nation. His progress to the capital and assumption of the presidency was marked by huge popular demonstrations, a kind of collective delirium hitherto unknown in Ecuador: 'You couldn't show me another revolution in the world as original as this one,' he said afterwards. 'All Ecuador united for this revolution: the Red united with the conservative, the priest with the soldier, the women and the man, the university student and the labourer – everyone made the glorious May Revolution.'

Early expectations that a profound change was about to take place in Ecuador were soon dashed. Velasco's obsession with the need to restore 'morality' to the country had little meaning for the vast majority struggling to survive in conditions of unemployment, inflation and high prices. A hunger march in Guayaquil at Christmas 1945 was brutally repressed by the police. His supporters began to fall out with each other, and many of them turned out to be less interested in revolution than in jobs in the bureaucracy. It became clear that the entrenched economic power of the elite was too great for him to resist, even if he genuinely wanted to. A series of business frauds and scandals which rocked the country went unpunished by the government. In the face of the renewed discontent and the incapacity of his government, Velasco Ibarra again (1946) declared himself dictator and began to persecute 'bolsheviks' and 'terrorists'. This was insufficient to make the economic and political crisis go away, however, and in 1947 the army overthrew him and installed a more suitable member of the elite in the presidential palace. Significantly, there was no popular reaction in Velasco's favour.

The 'Democratic Parenthesis' and Renewed Instability, 1948-72

An unexpected 12 years of political stability, the 'democratic parenthesis', followed the turmoils of the 1930s and 1940s, and a record three presidents in a row (Galo Plaza, 1948-52; Velasco Ibarra, 1952-56; Camilo Ponce, 1956-60) were elected normally and completed their constitutional terms of office. The underlying reason for this exceptional period of stability was to be found in a boom in the export economy, and the resulting prosperity and expansion of the Ecuadorean state. Firstly there was a vigorous recovery in a traditional export product, coffee. Exports of this rose from 10.7 million kilos in 1945 to 20.2 million kilos in 1950 and 32.3 million kilos in 1960. Another traditional export, cocoa, which had been in the doldrums ever since the First World War, also staged a limited recovery from 16.8 million kilos in 1945 to 26.7 million kilos in 1950 and 36.3 million kilos in 1960. Secondly, the postwar years saw the rapid growth of a new export product, bananas, which for a time dominated the economy. In 1945 Ecuadorean banana exports amounted to only 17,799 tons and accounted for less than one per cent of exports. In 1950 they amounted to 169,625 tons, rising to 895,053 tons in 1960 by which time they accounted for nearly two-thirds of exports. Although the annual harvest exceeded one million tons in 1963, the relative importance of bananas to the export economy declined in the second half of the 1960s to around 45 per cent.

Riding on the banana boom, the total value of Ecuador's exports rose from 40 million dollars in 1948 to 120 million dollars in 1960. This not only brought expansion and prosperity to producers and merchants on the coast where most of the new estates were located, it also brought a large growth in the income of the state. This meant that the governments of the 'democratic parenthesis' had much more to

17

spend. They had much more to buy off opposition and everyone could get a more generous slice of the cake than in the 1930s. Predictably enough, the major beneficiaries of government generosity were the elites, but there were some benefits, too, for the people. In 1947 the expenditure budget was 402.8 million *sucres*, of which 34.1 per cent went on education, welfare and public works, 25.2 per cent on the armed forces and police and 4.5 per cent on the public debt. In 1960 the expenditure budget was 2.1 billion *sucres*, of which 27.9 per cent went on education, welfare and public works, 19.6 per cent on armed forces and police and 10.3 per cent on the public debt.

However, the factors that underpinned the stability of the late 1940s and 1950s also set in motion forces which worked away under the surface of politics and eventually closed the parenthesis and opened a new period of crisis and instability. In the first place, the vast new wealth the state now had at its disposal led – especially under Galo Plaza – to ambitious development programmes, colonisation projects, construction and improvement of means of communication and transport and technical assistance for the development of natural resources. Galo Plaza was Ecuador's first modern *desarrollista* (developmentalist) president and the policies he pursued gave a greatly enhanced and strengthened role to the Ecuadorean state and to the bureaucratic middle class which ran it, at the expense of other members of the elite coalition which ran the country. In the second place, the coffee and banana industries which set the pace and tone for the Ecuadorean export economy in this period started to take on a different character from the traditional agro-exporting industries of the pre-war era. Unlike the sprawling, inefficiently-run *latifundia* (large estates) of the highlands or of the coast in former times, Ecuadorean coffee and banana estates tended to be well-capitalised and run on comparatively sophisticated lines technically. Moreover, unlike the huge enclaves of the multinational banana companies in Central America, Ecuadorean banana growers tended to be quite small-scale individual cultivators closely linked with the urban capitalists who invested in them.

As a result an incipient modernising capitalist class emerged in Ecuador, linked with the commercial and banking elite. Its rise was at the expense of the landed elite if they failed to adapt, while the peasants were forced to make a living from small, infertile plots of land or *minifundia*.

At the end of the 1950s the good times came to an end, and the failure of the governments of the 'parenthesis' to carry through structural reforms and eliminate Ecuadorean dependence on agricultural exports became manifest. Growth slackened off, the

TO: 1 Amwell Street, London EC1R 1UL
Telephone 071-278 2829

WRITE FOR A FREE 20-page CATALOGUE

Please send me a free catalogue
of Latin America Bureau books.
I am interested in books on
(please tick box/es):

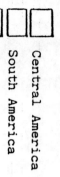

☐ Central America

☐ South America

☐ The Caribbean

NAME ....

ADDRESS ....

....

....

....

Latin America Bureau

Research and action on Latin America
and the Caribbean

Title of book in
which you found this
catalogue request
slip:

economy slid into recession, wages fell and consumer prices started to rise sharply. In this climate Velasco Ibarra, once more offering himself as the apostle of the 'rabble' against the rich and privileged, and taking a strong nationalist and anti-American line on the Cuban Revolution, won a comfortable victory. But just as in the 1940s, his *personalismo* and moralising style offended the elite and his inability to offer the popular classes a genuine solution to their problems offended his mass supporters. Finally, when students and workers came out on the streets in protest against him, he tried to resort to repression and was forced to resign in favour of his supposedly more left-wing Vice-President Carlos Julio Arosemena.

Arosemena immediately became the target of a campaign orchestrated by conservatives and the Central Intelligence Agency (CIA) (fully and carefully documented by one of the agents, Philip Agee, who later defected from the CIA and published his experiences, see Appendix 3). In 1963, Arosemena's indecorous personal behaviour – he was incapably drunk at a formal reception for the Chilean President and on other public occasions, once received a visiting mission in his bathrobe, had a penchant for visiting sleazy bars and shooting at the waiters, and finally insulted the American ambassador and the chairman of the American shipping company, Grace Line, at a banquet – provided the military with the pretext to intervene and expel him.

A brief period of military rule ensued from 1963 to 1966. The task of the junta, as they and their civilian supporters in the bureaucratic middle class saw it, was to hold the line against the 'communist threat' posed by the Cuban revolution, and to carry out necessary reforms of a modernising capitalist type in Ecuador. Although they succeeded in the first aim, they failed in the second. An agrarian reform law was passed in 1964 with the object of encouraging agricultural production and hence exports. As it did nothing about the *minifundia* and was resisted by the large landholders who disliked any interference in their affairs, it achieved very little beyond the abolition of *precarismo* (service tenure) – which actually aggravated the flight from the countryside to the towns. An attempt to reorganise the tax and tariff system on imports and exports, so as to increase government revenues, met with bitter opposition from the commercial elite of the coast. By 1966 the 'communist threat' had receded sufficiently for the elites to feel that they no longer needed the protection of the military. At the same time, popular resentment at their economic policies led to a wave of strikes and demonstrations by workers and students which forced the junta from power. Shortly after their departure, it was discovered that they had signed a secret protocol with the US abandoning Ecuador's claim to regulate fishing within the 200-mile maritime limit.

New elections were held in 1968 and Velasco Ibarra, the ageing idol of the urban sub-proletariat, won, to ascend to the presidency for the fifth and last time. Just as in his earlier terms, so in this one he showed himself incapable of tackling in any realistic way the urgent social and economic problems his supporters and the country faced. And, just as before, he proved incapable of imposing himself on the elites, whom he denounced when out of power, but when in power tried to conciliate. His instinct for authoritarian methods once more came to the fore and in the face of further waves of popular protest, demonstrations and strikes, he tried to make himself dictator. As on earlier occasions, this was too much for the military and the middle class, and in 1972 he was overthrown and replaced by a new military junta. By this time a new factor, which held out the possibility of escaping dependence on agricultural exports and transforming the country, was emerging: Ecuador was on the verge of becoming a major oil producer.

2. The Petroleum Generals

The Ecuadorean economy entered a new era when production from the *Oriente* oilfields came on stream and the country became a net exporter of petroleum. The oil export boom coincided with a dramatic increase in world oil prices, and initiated a period of economic growth that promised to transform the nature of Ecuadorean politics and society. The oil boom was also different in significant ways from previous commodity booms. In the past – even under a development-oriented President like Galo Plaza during the banana boom – the state had played a relatively modest role in economic life, partly due to its dependence on customs duties and taxes levied on an unstable foreign trade sector. The revenues from petroleum exports, by contrast, were not only vastly larger but accrued directly to the state. State control of petroleum revenues allowed it to play a more active role and pursue a set of social and economic goals with less fear of opposition from the traditional economic elites. In effect, such was the wealth generated by petroleum, that the prize for whichever group controlled the government was colossal, and elite opposition to reform could be bought off if necessary.

It is not surprising that the military seized power at this crucial moment in the country's history. Three factors impelled them to act: the deteriorating internal political situation, the impact of external examples, and oil policy.

To the military, the prospect that the oil wealth would be managed by what many in the armed forces regarded as corrupt and inefficient politicians served as a justification for its intervention. It also seemed likely that as the Velasco Ibarra government became more and more unpopular, a coup would be favourably received by public opinion. Velasco assumed dictatorial powers in June 1970 amidst severe balance of payments difficulties and escalating budget deficits. But the measures he took to combat the gathering economic crisis, closure

21

of the Congress, repression of his opponents, large tax increases, devaluation of the currency – soon removed the last vestiges of support for the old *caudillo*.

At first the military gave their backing to the man they had deposed so often before. They were reluctant to take direct control because unhappy memories of the 1963-66 experience of military rule were still strong. Moreover, a rift had opened up between the traditionalists and a group of progressive younger officers who were impressed by the reforms being carried out by a military government in neighbouring Peru. Finally, many nationalist officers supported Velasco's strong stand in defending the claim for a 200-mile maritime limit against the incursions of Californian tuna fishermen and imposing heavy fines on unlicensed vessels. The military, in other words, lacked the necessary institutional unity and preparedness to take power immediately.

Although traditionally suspicious of Velasco, therefore, the military at first supported his austerity package to tackle the deteriorating economic situation. The uneasy truce between the President and the armed forces did not last long. The first signs of disaffection surfaced when a group of officers led by General Luis Jacomé Chávez rebelled against Defence Minister Jorge Acosta Velasco, the President's nephew and admirer of the Peruvian experiment. General Jacomé accused Acosta of using his position to promote young radical officers into key posts. Jacomé also represented the Guayaquil business interests who were disgruntled by the higher taxes levied on exporters and plantation owners. It took the conciliation skills of the head of the War College, General Guillermo Rodríguez Lara, to engineer a compromise on the basis of the removal of both Acosta and the armed forces chief.

The anxiety of the officers increased as the presidential election of 1972 approached, and it seemed that the winner of what was turning into a divisive and bitter campaign would be the erratic Guayaquil populist Assad Bucaram. Both Velasco, who resented Bucaram as the young pretender to his constituency among the Guayaquil proletariat, and the military, who regarded the CFP leader as a dangerous and unpredictable leftist, were determined to block his candidacy. Velasco tried to undermine his rival's credibility by twice expelling him from the country and casting doubt on his Ecuadorean citizenship. In such a situation the military could pose as the upholders of law and order in the face of the prospect of chaos caused by a protracted dispute over Bucaram's candidacy.

External events influenced the armed forces in their decision to intervene. Both the national and reformist model of military rule as practised in Peru and the repressive right-wing Brazilian solution had

Asaad Bucaram

Known affectionately as 'Don Buca' by his followers in Guayaquil's *suburbios*, Asaad Bucaram was a rarity among Ecuador's political elite: a man of humble origins (he started adult life as a travelling salesman for a textile company) and limited education who became one of his country's most powerful politicians. First elected to Congress in 1958, he soon distinguished himself by his forceful approach to political debate (provoking fist-fights and brandishing a pistol at heated moments of congressional sessions). He seized control of the Guayaquil-based populist party, the CFP, in the early 1960s and dominated coastal politics as its *director supremo*. His inflammatory oratory and unpredictable politics (to the right he was a Marxist, to the left a fascist demagogue) earned him the implacable hatred of opponents who referred to him contemptuously as *el turco* (the Turk).

Under Bucaram's leadership the CFP became his personal political vehicle, failing to develop a coherent ideology or national organisation and showing little interest in structural change. He surrounded himself with loyal but mediocre 'yes men' and often employed gangs of thugs to intimidate his opponents. Twice elected as mayor of Guayaquil, he was arrested and exiled four times between 1963 and 1972 by the military, who distrusted him, and his arch-rival for the populist vote, Velasco Ibarra.

In both 1972 and 1978 Bucaram emerged as the frontrunner for the presidency. Only military intervention, in the first case, and legal skulduggery robbed him of the prize. Born of Lebanese immigrant parents shortly after their arrival in the country, he could not comply with the stipulation that they had to be Ecuadorean citizens at the time of his birth. He died in November 1981.

their supporters and advocates within the Ecuadorean officer corps. At the time of the 1972 coup, the Peruvian model of military-directed change enjoyed considerable prestige throughout Latin America and seemed to offer a non-violent alternative to the now-discredited civilian reformism of the 1960s. However, there was an important difference between the Ecuadorean military and their Peruvian counterparts. In Peru, a determined group of radical officers was able to organise a government that, initially at least, maintained internal cohesion. In Ecuador, the corresponding group was too small and divided to do the same. In fact, it was not so much a desire to carry out a reform programme, as a concern to safeguard the unity and cohesion of the armed forces against the attempts of civilian politicians to politicise them and harness them to their own ambitions, that triggered the intervention. Because the Ecuadorean officer corps, unlike the Peruvian or Brazilian, failed to resolve the internal debate

23

one way or the other, the military government they installed in 1972 lacked clear definitions of its policies and was uncertain about the nature of the political project it was supposed to be pursuing.

On one issue, however, all factions of the military were united. They were determined to ensure that they kept control over the substantial revenues about to be generated from the exploitation of the country's oil wealth. The discovery by the Texaco-Gulf consortium of large, exploitable deposits of oil at Lago Agrio in the *Oriente* region excited widespread expectations about a forthcoming bonanza. The military were determined that a substantial portion of these revenues should be allocated to arms purchases, salary increases and enhancement of their 'national security' role. During the previous decade they had steadily expanded their involvement in economic and political affairs. Officers became accustomed to serve as ministers as well as central and local government officials. Their training programmes were widened to include courses in administration, economic policy and policing as well as more conventional military skills. The armed forces operated their own airline (TAME), merchant marine (TRASNAVE), tanker fleet (FLOPEC) and shipyards (ASTINAVE), acquired land for housing and rural colonisation schemes, and set up their own farming, retailing and import-export enterprises. Quite naturally, they saw the oilfields and their installations in strategic terms and took a close interest in all aspects of oil policy.

Two features of Velasco's oil policy particularly disturbed the joint military command. One was the delay in signing a contract to build a state refinery in order to eliminate costly dependence on foreign-owned processes. The other was the avalanche of concessions granted to foreign oil companies to explore for petroleum under Ecuador's liberal regulations. By 1972 nearly all the potential oil bearing land in the *Oriente* had been handed over to the companies on very favourable terms and a highly dubious deal struck with the ADA company to exploit an offshore field. Dissatisfaction with Velasco's 1971 Hydrocarbons Law was widespread. While it apparently paved the way for greater state and national control over the industry, it did not apply to existing investments and only affected companies entering the industry after the year 2010. By the time the military took control, a general consensus existed that there was a need to revise the generous and one-sided relationship with the international oil companies.

The political orientation of the military government which bundled Velasco out of the presidency during the Carnival of 1972 seemed to signal a shift to the left in economic and social policy. The leader of the coup, General Rodríguez Lara, proclaimed a 'revolutionary and

Ecuador's military ruler: General Rodríguez Lara

Nicknamed *bombita* (the little bomb), Guillermo Rodríguez Lara came from Pujili, a small town in Cotopaxi province, the kind of highland background which has long been typical of the Ecuadorean officer corps. A landowner and self-made man, he rose quickly through the ranks of the army. Like most of his contemporaries, Rodríguez received his training abroad; in Colombia, at the US military training school in the Panama Canal Zone, and Fort Leavenworth, Kansas. Because of this background he was considered to be pro-US. His skills as a conciliator brought him to the fore in army politics and he showed considerable political ability in maintaining the loyalty of the notoriously dissent-ridden armed forces for almost four years. As a politician Rodríguez favoured the traditional populist style, attacking foreign capitalists, the oligarchy and corrupt politicians and bureaucrats. Like Velasco Ibarra, he travelled widely throughout the country and revealed a penchant for lengthy speeches. When he was deposed in 1976 he returned to his home town to a rapturous welcome.

nationalist' government that would 'transform the country's basic structures to make possible a dynamic and effective programme that will fully benefit the whole community and those who, until now, have been less favoured'. The new government – 'the little colonels who've been reading Lenin and Mao Tse-tung' snorted Velasco from his last exile in Buenos Aires – promised an 'effective' agrarian reform, a more equitable tax structure, a reduction in social and regional inequalities through a programme of housing, education, health care and public works, an end to corrupt public administration, and the regulation and control of foreign capital. The goals of the programme were set out in the Integral Plan of Transformation and Development, 1973-77, an idealistic but vague document located very much in the Ecuadorean populist tradition, promising benefits for all without specifiying what, if any, sacrifices would be necessary. Development was to be promoted by 'sowing petroleum' which would provide the investment capital for the government's ambitious plans to build up infrastructure and agricultural, industrial and social projects. The success of the Plan depended on skilled management and decision-making – the very qualities the military government did not have at its disposal, since Rodríguez Lara moved quickly to remove any colleague who threatened his predominant position or acted independently. By purging strong personalities from his cabinet the President ensured that there were few challenges to his authority, but it also meant that crucial decisions were often subject to lengthy delays and compromises.

25

Oil:the nationalist phase

The man chosen to implement the 'nationalist' oil policy was Captain (later Rear-Admiral) Gustavo Jarrín Ampudia. Although, like his ministerial colleagues, he had no previous knowledge of the oil industry, the new Minister of Natural Resources represented those sections of the navy that had been radicalised by the fishing limits dispute with the US, and soon managed to recruit a team of left-wing technocrats who were sympathetic to his nationalist line. It was a propitious moment to adopt such a policy. The oil had already been discovered and the investments made, so the bargaining initiative lay with the host government. Moreover, Ecuador could draw on the experience of Venezuela and Middle East OPEC countries which had taken advantage of the oil crisis brought on by the 1973 Arab-Israeli War to increase government participation in their industries. Domestic opinion was also flowing strongly in favour of the nationalist case following the publication of Jaime Galarza's best-selling *Festín del Petróleo*, a stinging indictment of corruption and mismanagement by the oil companies.

The first step towards the reassertion of national sovereignty was the issue of Decree 430 (6 June 1972), under which the majority of exploration concessions reverted to the Ecuadorean state and the companies were obliged to renegotiate their contracts. Later the same month a state oil corporation, the *Corporación Estatal Petrolera Ecuatoriana* (CEPE) was created with responsibility for marketing, exploration, refining and, eventually, production. Jarrín's clear aim was to wrest as much territory as possible from the oil companies and entrust it to CEPE for long-term development. After more than a year of negotiations, an agreement was signed with Texaco-Gulf, the largest of the foreign consortia operating in Ecuador. Jarrín struck a hard bargain. The concession period on Texaco's remaining blocks was reduced from 40 to 20 years, a new regime of taxes, rents and royalties was brought into effect, and CEPE was given the right to buy into the consortium with a 25 per cent stake.

The nationalists seemed to reinforce their position when Ecuador joined OPEC as a full member in November 1973. Shortly afterwards, Jarrín became President of the organisation and used his influence to press for higher prices and greater state participation in production. At this point, however, he began to come under mounting domestic criticism from conservatives who accused him of xenophobia and being under communist influence, and demanded that he abandon his hard-line approach. The Right questioned the value of OPEC membership and the wisdom of ordering the companies to cut

26

An oil pipeline.

The navy's oil nationalist: Captain Jarrín

A former head of the Naval Academy, where he advocated a radical 'national security' ideology, Gustavo Jarrín Ampudia was appointed to the key post of Natural Resources Minister in 1972. He created CEPE, the state oil company modelled on Brazil's Petrobrás. Adopting a strategy of gradual oil nationalisation, he masterminded CEPE's 25 per cent purchase of Texaco-Gulf, began the construction of the Esmeraldas oil refinery and groomed CEPE to take over the supply of the domestic market. He took Ecuador into OPEC and Quito began to enjoy international status as a venue for Third World conferences. In a speech to the United Nations in April 1974 Jarrín spoke of the oil struggle as 'only a chapter in the battle undertaken by the developing nations for the establishment of control and sovereignty in the exploitation of their resources'. As a military elitist who found it difficult to establish strong links with civilian politicians, and as a naval man in a military-political structure which gave pre-eminence to the army, Jarrín was unable to build up a power base within the armed forces. He soon had the oil companies baying for his blood, and Rodríguez Lara was only too pleased to dismiss a man who had acquired the status of a 'superminister'. In October 1974 Jarrin was dispatched abroad to serve as naval attaché at the London embassy.

production, as a conservation measure, at a time when oil prices were rising steadily. They argued that Ecuador should be free to fix its own selling price to suit conditions prevailing in the international market rather than be bound by agreements dictated as much by the Middle East conflict as by economic criteria. Jarrín's counter-argument was that it made more sense to leave the oil in the ground and wait for the completion of a new refinery at Esmeraldas so that the country would not always have to import costly refined petroleum. The argument was really a more sophisticated version of the old debate about whether the country should simply export the raw materials it was endowed with at whatever price it could command, or whether it should try and process them and gain the benefit of the 'value-added'.

The oil companies intervened in the debate by boycotting new exploration bids and putting the blame on Ecuador's overzealous nationalism. This gave ammunition to Jarrín's critics, who could now point out that the only achievement of the nationalist oil policy had been to drive Amoco, Shenandoah and Sun Oil out of the *Oriente* and leave Texaco with the ability to paralyse the country's oil exports whenever it wished. The US added to the oil companies' pressure, firstly by excluding Ecuador, along with other OPEC members, from a preference scheme in the new Trade Act, then by trying to shift the balance of opinion within the military by threatening to cut off military aid if Jarrín remained in office. In a last defiant move the minister dismissed the 'imperialist threats' and demanded that CEPE take a 51 per cent stake in Texaco-Gulf. But the odds were now stacked against the nationalists. The recession in the economies of the developed countries reduced the demand for oil and tipped the scales in favour of the companies. These now had the support of conservative interests demanding the abandonment of nationalist policies and a return to civilian rule. In October 1974 Jarrín was dismissed and the proposal to take a majority share in Texaco-Gulf was shelved. The anti-nationalist offensive had claimed its first victim.

The consortium immediately moved to consolidate its victory and step up the pressure on the military government. An investment and export boycott was justified on the grounds that Ecuadorean crude oil was too expensive to find buyers in the world market. Faced with the threat of a slump in oil revenues (production in the first half of 1975 was only half of what it had been in the corresponding period in 1974) and an imminent budget crisis and balance of payments deficit, the government caved in. In July 1975 the new Minister of Natural Resources, Luis Salazar Landet, announced a reduction of 43 cents a barrel in the price of Ecuadorean oil. The 1975 crisis had forced the government to accept an uncomfortable reality, and punctured forever the euphoria which surrounded the early boom years when oil seemed to be the panacea for all the country's economic ills. When oil revenues soared, so did public expenditure as Ecuador, like other oil producers, looked to develop its economy as rapidly as possible. The events of 1975 spelled out the brutal truth that, for Ecuador, ambitious and costly development plans were just as much at the mercy of external markets and just as dependent on the whim of powerful foreign companies as they had ever been in the age of agricultural commodity exports.

Industrial Development

The influx of petro-dollars began a period of economic expansion in which the industrial sector was to play an important role. The 1973 five-year development plan aimed to create a modern industrial sector by encouraging import substitution, expanding the internal market and diversifying the range of exports. Rodríguez Lara's project was essentially a national capitalist one in which an alliance of the state and the private sector would sponsor development and modernisation. The project, however, rested on some questionable

29

assumptions. Amongst them was the belief that it was possible to forge an alliance with a group of progressive national entrepreneurs, and that these new dynamic modernisers would split decisively away from the traditional agricultural exporting elite. Moreover, the model relied heavily on continuing membership of international (such as OPEC) and regional (such as the Andean Common Market) organisations, so as to reinforce Ecuador's negotiating position with transnational capital. This way, it was thought, the inevitable growth of foreign investment implied by the development plan would not lead the country further down the slippery slope of external dependency.

The absence of an autonomous industrial class meant that the state played an increasingly active role in promoting economic development. Numerous state agencies and corporations were established to administer the injection of oil wealth into the economy and petroleum revenues were increasingly earmarked for an array of public sector enterprises. Apart from the state oil corporation CEPE, which received 13 per cent of all such revenues between 1975 and 1983, the government created a state telephone and telegraph monopoly (*Instituto Ecuatoriano de Telecomunicaciones*, IETEL), channelled some ten per cent of petroleum income into the electricity corporation INECEL, and bailed out ailing companies including the national airline, *Ecuatoriana de Aviación*. Public financial institutions were another channel for investment into the economy. The Central Bank (*Banco Central del Ecuador*, CE) was joined by specialised banking and credit corporations for agriculture (*Banco Nacional de Fomento*, BNF), industry (*Corporación Financiera Nacional*, CFN) and public sector institutions (*Banco Ecuatoriano de Desarrollo Económico*, BEDE).

There was no objection at first from the private sector, which was happy to see the resuscitation of lame duck industries when the declared aim was to return them to private ownership. The prospect of competition from state enterprises, however, was quite a different matter and elicited a hostile response. When the military established their own industrial and commercial ventures in the shape of engineering companies, and their airline TAME began to compete directly with the private sector, a heated argument over the role of the state in the economy began to rage.

León Febres Cordero, the combative President of the Guayaquil chamber of industry and head of the Noboa group of companies (on account of whose extensive sugar interests he was at one time nicknamed the 'Baron of Sugar'), spearheaded the criticism of the state's new entrepreneurial role. His objections focussed particularly on the activities of the *Superintendencia de Precios*, an office set up to control the prices of industrial and agricultural products, and on the marketing agencies ENPROVIT and ENAC; these, he claimed, were interfering with market forces and stifling private enterprise. The loudest protests against the government's policies came from Guayaquil. Here on the coast, there was an added dimension of regionalist resentment at the growth of the state bureaucracy which meant jobs for well-connected highlanders up in Quito; they also complained of 'excessive centralisation'.

Although they were now the recipients of generous state incentives and protection in the form of subsidies and low interest rates, the industrialists became increasingly critical of government policy, especially on agrarian reform and oil. The independent national capitalist class, the dynamic modernisers whom the military expected to emerge in response to the new opportunities, failed to appear. Instead the major beneficiaries were wealthy exporters and landowners who had resources enough and were quick-witted enough to diversify their interests. The new industrial entrepreneurs were often linked socially through family connections with the traditional dominant classes. By appropriating the development plans of the military, they were able to prevent the regime from building up a strong political base for its economic project. The military government remained vulnerable to those forces which aimed to dilute or undermine its strategy.

Foreign Investment

Before the 1970s Ecuador was only of marginal interest to foreign investors, and the capital that did enter the country was destined mainly for export agriculture. The advent of the oil boom transformed this situation. Within a short time the country's healthy financial situation, the improvements in infrastructure resulting from state investment in communications and energy projects, and the growing regional and domestic market, created attractive possibilities for foreign capital. From 1970 to 1976 foreign participation in manufacturing industry grew more than fivefold (60 million dollars to 220 million dollars). Besides petroleum, foreign capital invested heavily in food and drink, chemicals, electrical goods and car assembly, and by 1976 transnationals owned or controlled 14 of Ecuador's largest companies.

At first the industrial sector benefited from the inflow of foreign capital, from the Industrial Development Law which encouraged the import of raw materials, machinery and equipment, and from the

31

preferential treatment given to industry under the Andean Pact. Soon, however, the negative effects of this type of dependent industrialisation became apparent. The heavy reliance on inputs of foreign capital and technology brought on a deteriorating trade balance and growing foreign indebtedness. Instead of reducing the level of dependence, foreign penetration of the Ecuadorean economy increased dramatically under the stimulus of the liberal investment laws and the willingness of the government to ignore the Andean Pact's rules for regulating foreign investment in the commercial and financial sectors. Nor did this kind of industrial development do anything to improve the living standards of the masses. Much of the investment was capital intensive and failed to tackle the twin problems of unemployment and low consumer purchasing power. New investment simply reinforced the concentration of wealth and exaggerated regional disparities by boosting economic activity in the two growth poles of Quito and Guayaquil.

The contrast between the beneficiaries of the boom and the rest of the population was stark. In 1975, the World Bank estimated that 65 per cent of the rural population were living below the poverty line while a quarter of the population controlled 70 per cent of the nation's wealth. The shortage of work in the cities and the acceleration of migration from the impoverished countryside created a rapidly-growing urban informal sector, in which growing numbers of people (45 per cent of the urban employed in 1974, more than 55 per cent in 1980, with black spots like the slums of Guayaquil where as many as 75 per cent of the population are in this sector) struggled to survive by improvised, insecure and often dangerous or unhealthy semi-jobs, without prospects or security. Nowhere are the inequities of the development process more apparent than in the cities. During the boom years of the early 1970s, Ecuador witnessed an orgy of imports and conspicuous consumption by the urban middle and upper income groups. Expensive cars, stereos and other luxury items, benefiting from lower import duties, poured into the country while the civil and military bureaucracies indulged themselves with prestige office blocks, new equipment and other status symbols. Ultimately the bill for this unrestrained consumption could only be met by borrowing abroad.

The military government's programme to stimulate industrial development achieved quite impressive results if it is borne in mind that at the onset of the period of growth, Ecuador had one of the smallest industrial sectors in Latin America. The total value of manufacturing output quadrupled between 1970 and 1976 and hundreds of new firms were registered under the Industrial

Development Law. From 1972 to the end of the decade, manufacturing industry registered annual growth rates of 10 per cent in real terms and industrial employment expanded at an annual average rate of 11.5 per cent during the mid-1970s. But there were two fatal flaws in the industrial edifice. Firstly, industrial growth depended on external demand and the purchasing power of the numerically small middle and upper classes. Industrialists were not interested in redistribution policies designed to create a mass consumer market, they preferred a close association with the multinationals and the cocoon of state protectionism. Secondly, by 1978 almost half the entire central government budget was being swallowed by exemptions and subsidies on oil, basic foods and credits. The programme could only be sustained by borrowing, eventually incurring crippling debt service payments. By 1980 debt servicing stood at nearly 23 per cent of total expenditure.

Agrarian Reform

Significant changes had already occurred in the agricultural sector in the 1960s. The archaic labour system of *huasipungo* (a form of service tenancy) had disappeared. In the highlands the large estates had restructured and commercialised their operations in response to urban consumer demand for meat and dairy products. On the coast new crops – soya, African palm, cotton and hemp – were added to the traditional cultivation of bananas, cocoa, coffee and rice. These developments, however, had done little to alleviate the problems of a perrennial shortage of basic foodstuffs for popular consumption, or the inefficiency of *minifundia* production, or the low levels of mechanisation and the existence of a large surplus of landless labourers. The attempts at agrarian reform of the 1963-66 military government had actually aggravated some of these problems.

Renewal of the agrarian reform figured as an important part of Rodríguez Lara's national development plan, but as in 1964, peasant hopes were raised only to be dashed against the rock of the landowners' intransigent opposition. The Agricultural Chambers of the coast and highlands joined forces to emasculate the proposals through a campaign that included threats to withhold taxes and warnings that the 'Sovietisation' of agriculture would have dire consequences for output. The right strategy, as they saw it, was to colonise the *Oriente*, using it as an outlet for the excess rural population. When the long-delayed provisions of the new Agrarian Reform Law became public (October 1973), they bore the

33

The slow progress of agrarian reform

Period	Agrarian Reform (total hectares)	Colonisation (total hectares)
1964-66	85,601	207,266
1967-71	93,291	286,947
1972-77	251,668	713,115
Total	430,500	1,207,329

Source: H Handelman, 'Ecuadorean Agrarian Reform: the politics of limited change' in *Politics of Agrarian Change* (Indiana University Press, 1981),p.73

The 1973 Agrarian Reform Law stressed increased production rather than land redistribution. It reassured private farmers that they would not lose efficiently farmed land. In fact, land could only be expropriated if:
- the principal activity of the owner is not farming
- less than 80 per cent of the area is under cultivation
- it is inefficiently farmed
- it is farmed by squatters without legal title
- it is in an area of 'great demographic pressure'

Despite receiving an increased budget in the 1970s, the *Instituto Ecuatoriano de Reforma Agraria y Colonización*, (Agrarian Reform Institute, IERAC) made little progress towards a genuine agrarian reform because of the vague wording of the Law and the high cost of the compensation offered. Overly bureaucratic, IERAC's procedures were cumbersome and slow, suffering from a shortage of trained personnel and lacking the resources to provide credits and technical assistance to the recipients of land. Theoretically more than two million hectares were subject to expropriation; in practice, less than half a million had been redistributed by 1978, and of this 20 per cent was former church lands. Up to 1980 less than 20 per cent of the peasants and less than 15 per cent of the land had been affected by agrarian reform. Recently IERAC claimed that, during the 20 years since 1964, 737,676 hectares were expropriated, benefiting 79,000 people. Colonisation in the eastern Amazon of 2.26 million hectares benefited 51,785 people. IERAC's director Rafael Pérez Reyna claimed these figures represented 'a giant step without precedence in the history of Ecuador'.

unmistakable stamp of another intense campaign of lobbying by the landowners.

The new law emphasised efficient production and provision of credit rather than the land redistribution and social justice called for by peasant spokesmen. It contained soothing phrases about respect for private property and omitted any mention of a maximum area of 'productively cultivated units' that could be privately owned. Land expropriation, a long and complicated legal process, took second place to the provision of credits, state subsidies and the import of agricultural machinery and fertilisers. Although more than 20,000 families did benefit from the half million hectares converted to agricultural use by the Agrarian Reform Institute (IERAC) between 1972 and 1975, this was only a tiny proportion of the rural population and the bulk of the land on which they were settled came from colonisation projects rather than redistribution. Much of the inefficiently farmed land was quite unaffected by the reform.

Timid as the reform programme was, the landowners waged a vigorous campaign against it. They obtained the dismissal of the Agriculture Minister, Guillermo Maldonado Lince, whom they branded a 'communist' for suggesting that, in some cases, even well-cultivated land might be subject to expropriation if it served a 'social function'. Then they undermined the government's price control machinery, which had been imposed in an effort to curb spiralling food prices, by hoarding or smuggling their produce over the borders into Colombia or Peru and so circumventing the state marketing system. By 1977 the pretence that the reform had a redistributive function had been abandoned and the government was on the defensive. The landowning elite, using a combination of political pressure, economic sabotage and violent thuggery which included the murder of peasant union leaders, had their way. Faced with the prospect of mounting food shortages, and their incalculable social consequences, the government introduced the agricultural promotion law (1979) which gave precedence to raising productivity and increasing efficiency on existing farms. The large landowners predictably took the lion's share of the benefits available, leaving smallholders starved of credits and technical assistance. The produce from the large capitalist *haciendas*, however, did little to ease the domestic food crisis. They increasingly switched their activities to profitable export crops and premium dairy products such as cheese, which were far beyond the means of the poor to buy.

The effects of the injection of capital were rather different on the coast. Here, the formation of rice-producing cooperatives on relatively high quality land brought a capitalist ethos into agriculture but with the state replacing the *hacendado* (estate owner) by setting prices and buying the bulk of the crop. Yet the number of peasants involved in these was quite small and the coastal landowners, like their compatriots in the highlands, successfully repelled the threat of expropriation. By the end of the decade, less than seven per cent of the cultivable land on the coast had been subject to the agrarian reform.

35

Small-scale rural sugar extraction.

As a result subsistence agriculture has stagnated and nothing has been done to assist the large number of peasants with economically unviable smallholdings of a hectare or less.

The only escape from rural poverty for the landless peasant has been migration to the cities; this, combined with the high rate of population growth, has meant that Ecuador became the most rapidly urbanising society in Latin America for a time in the 1970s. The population of the capital more than doubled in ten years and one estimate has put urban population growth for Ecuador as a whole at 140 per cent between 1960 and 1980. However, as the country also had one of the continent's highest proportions of rural population, it was not until 1983 that urban levels passed the 50 per cent mark. In fact, the cities acted as a safety valve for the rural poor. While economic growth lasted they could find employment as cheap labour in the thriving construction industry and informal services sector. Rural migrants poured into the marginal suburbs of the larger urban centres in search of employment. But by 1980 the economic crisis had begun to bite, severely limiting job opportunities and bringing to an end the miniboom in agriculture based on higher urban consumption patterns. It is even less likely now that agrarian reform can provide a panacea for the chronic levels of under- and unemployment currently afflicting the workforce. The transformation of the large estates into capital-intensive enterprises requiring large tracts of pasture land means that redistribution is no longer on the political agenda of those in power.

The Fall of Rodríguez Lara

By 1975 the Ecuadorean economy was sliding into crisis as the consequences of the generals' policies began to manifest themselves. The oil companies' export boycott meant that oil revenues, which accounted for 60 per cent of government income, fell by almost half in the first six months of the year and precipitated a sharp deterioration in the balance of trade. The economic crisis coincided with a resurgence of civilian political activity and the formation of a *Frente Cívico* (Civic Front) made up of the main centre and right-wing parties who called for new elections to be held. The beleaguered government, without civilian allies, tried to blame the political disaffection on a plot hatched by the oil companies in collusion with the CIA.

There is little doubt that the US hoped to detach Ecuador from its commitment to OPEC and that conservative business interests favoured a swift return to civilian rule. It was at this point that the

37

military's failure to mobilise popular support behind its reformist project became crucial. The military's lack of ideological direction and the disagreements within the armed forces made it impossible to put together a popular constituency that might have counterbalanced the organised assault on them by the dominant classes. What popular support did exist had been eroded by inflation and the government's inability to control price rises. Isolated and exposed, Rodríguez Lara was subjected to mounting criticism from the chambers of industry and agriculture and demands for public spending cuts and an end to state intervention. Condemnation became more vigorous still when the government promulgated Decree 738 which imposed higher duties on selected 'non-essential' industrial and consumer imports.

Towards the end of 1975, the gathering political crisis broke. Under intense pressure from civilian politicians, a group of officers led by the army Chief of Staff, General Raúl González Alvear, tried to stage a coup d'etat. The 'funeral parlour revolt' – so-called because the plotters established their headquarters in a funeral parlour – was quickly put down with 22 dead and many more wounded. But although it failed because of poor planning, it brought sharply into focus two pointers to Rodríguez Lara's imminent political demise: the complete lack of popular support for the government and the deep rift within the ranks of the armed forces. Last ditch efforts to appease his critics by promising a return to civilian rule and amendment of Decree 738 could not salvage the President's position. In January 1976 he was relieved of office and replaced by a junta composed of the heads of the three armed services, General Guillermo Durán (Army), Admiral Alfredo Póveda (Navy) and General Luis Leoro (Air Force). The triumvirate, styling itself the *Consejo Supremo de Gobierno* (Supreme Council of Government), undertook to call elections during 1977.

Military Rule: the Second Phase, 1976-79

The removal of Rodríguez Lara marked the moment when the military government swung to the right and the conservatives within the military seized the ascendancy over the nationalists. Above all, it represented a victory for the business elite whose skilful use of the privately-owned mass media and personal contacts sowed the seeds of dissension inside the armed forces. But while their influence was undoubtedly on the wane, the nationalists maintained a foothold in the new administration through Colonel René Vargas Pazzos, the Minister of Natural Resources. Vargas ignored the press campaign against the CEPE and urged the complete nationalisation of Texaco-Gulf on the grounds that the consortium had failed to meet its investment and exploration targets. Rather than submit to pressure for further reductions in the oil price, Vargas favoured the formation of joint ventures between CEPE and foreign oil companies as the future model for the development of the industry.

It soon became clear that nationalist oil policies were not compatible with the triumvirate's pro-business orientation. Although Vargas pushed through the nationalisation of Gulf Oil's holdings in January 1977 after a long-drawn-out struggle, a month later he fell victim to the ambitions of the army chief. By replacing Vargas with a conservative, Durán consolidated his own power base and ingratiated himself with the business elite. Under the direction of the conservative Finance Minister, Santiago Sevilla (an open admirer of the Pinochet regime in Chile), economic policy shifted to the right and the junta launched a programme to create a more attractive climate for foreign investors and provide incentives for exporters. Confronted now with high inflation, escalating government expenditure and a deteriorating external situation, the junta tried to tighten its alliance with foreign capital and make itself respectable by pursuing anti-labour policies. The inevitable consequences of the austerity measures introduced after 1976 were an increase in unemployment and a reduction in living standards; the military found themselves resorting more and more to the use of repression to contain popular discontent and growing labour militancy.

Labour Fights Back

The Ecuadorean labour movement has traditionally been one of the smallest and weakest in Latin America. Before the 1970s the dominant classes were able to ignore or neutralise popular protest by the selective use of populist politics and coercion. The level of popular mobilisation is partly explained by the existence of pre-capitalist, artisanal forms of economic organisation and activity. The three major trade union confederations which made up the bulk of the formal labour movement (*Confederación de Trabajadores del Ecuador*, (CTE); *Confederación Ecuatoriana de Organizaciones Clasistas*, (CEDOC); *Confederación Ecuatoriana de Organizaciones Sindicales Libres*, (CEOSL)) were also weakened in varying degrees by factionalism, corruption and poor organisation. Union leaders often preferred to pursue personal and ideological rivalries rather than concentrate on advancing the interests of their members. Because of this, many workers opted to join the smaller and often very splintered occupational unions or artisanal associations, and resisted absorption into the big three confederations. The confederations had some success in organising and securing economic and social security benefits for the small factory-based working class, but made few inroads into the much larger numbers of the urban poor and the subproletariat. The low penetration of unionism in general was reflected in the growth of non-union forms of association, particularly artisan guilds, peasant and worker cooperatives and neighbourhood associations.

During the opening phases of military rule organised labour gained some benefits from the pro-industry and mildly redistributionist policies of a government which was aiming to create an enlarged domestic market. Encouraged by this situation, labour spokesmen, much to the alarm of the employers, began to make political as well as economic demands. Indeed, the upsurge in labour activity and the solidarity which the rival confederations occasionally achieved at this time was another factor behind the removal of Rodríguez Lara, who, the employers felt, was too soft on labour and incapable of disciplining the workforce.

Organised labour's new-found confidence and solidarity took the form of the creation of an umbrella organisation, the *Frente Unitario de Trabajadores* (FUT), to coordinate the actions of the three confederations, and the calling of a nationwide general strike in November 1975. This demonstrated their ability to mobilise mass support behind a nine-point programme of political and economic demands which included: (i) an increase in the minimum wage; (ii) an overall 50 per cent wage increase; (iii) indexation of pay to keep up with inflation; (iv) repeal of anti-labour laws; (v) nationalisation of strategic industries; (vi) a more radical agrarian reform; (vii) labour participation in state organisation; (viii) higher social spending; and (ix) the elimination of foreign influences.

Faced with this growing labour militancy, the alarmed employers tried to pin the blame for the economic crisis on 'greedy' trade unions, and undermine the FUT's credibility. In March 1976 the Pichincha Chamber of Industry, representing the industrialists of the capital, warned against 'the anarchy and disrespect afflicting worker-employer relations' which was being caused by the union's overtly 'political' campaigning. The junta reacted to this sign of employer discontent by banning political demonstrations and outlawing what Interior Minister Colonel Bolívar Jarrín called 'subversive activities, strikes and anti-government campaigns'. The hard-line Labour Minister, General Durán, did not hesitate to use strong-arm methods to end strikes and factory occupations. The most notorious clash to

40

occur under this new, tough policy took place at the El Aztra sugar mill in October 1977 when police forcibly evicted strikers occupying the plant, massacring around 100 people in the process. That same year, a confrontation between the government and the teachers' union, the UNE, culminated in the dissolution of the union and a two-year imprisonment of its president. This anti-labour offensive was masterminded by the Labour Ministry, which gave strong backing to employers during wage negotiations and gave recognition to less militant breakaway factions in an attempt to exploit the personal and political rivalries among union leaders.

By the middle of 1977, the crackdown on labour seemed to be having the desired effect. A combination of official harassment and inter-union splits meant that a second national strike, called by the FUT in May 1977, was only partially successful, and in 1978 the number of official labour disputes registered a 50 per cent drop against the 1975 figures. Some of the problems confronting the unions in this period were related to struggles over the political direction of the union movement.

In 1976 the Left gained control of CEDOC and came under revolutionary socialist influence, while the Christian Democrats formed their own CEDOC-CLAT.

During the dictatorship, then, the labour movement acquired a political voice and, in the absence of the outlawed political parties was able to present itself as the defender of working- class interests. This meant that, although generally in favour, some union leaders regarded the restoration of democracy and the return of the political parties as a mixed blessing, and were uneasy at the overtures being made to the unions by parties looking for union support for electoral purposes. They realised that the left-wing parties, to which many of them belonged, had never succeeded in mobilising and consistently keeping any significant support from the voters. There was little correlation between the level of unionisation and disciplined voting for left-wing candidates in national elections. They recognised that there was a low level of class consciousness among the urban workforce. This could partly be explained by their relatively recent incorporation into the wage economy as well as the limited absolute size of the factory proletariat, whose living standards had anyway been improving. In addition, populist politics continued to have an appeal for the urban masses. In such a situation, it might be argued, it would make more sense for the unions to concentrate on building up and consolidating their own structures, rather than dissipating their energies on behalf of the political parties.

3. Democracy Restored?

With a military government anxious to regulate and influence the outcome of the process of restoring democracy, the return to civilian rule was plagued by delays, rumours of coups and mounting popular disillusion. The unpopularity of the military reached new heights when conservative officers conspired with right-wing politicians to press for power to be handed over immediately to a constituent assembly. This would have given control over the electoral process to an institution with an inbuilt right-wing majority. However, the constitutionalists in the armed forces, led by Admiral Póveda and stiffened by a visit from President Carter's wife Rosalynn, managed to head off this manoeuvre.

The elections were at first scheduled for early 1978 and three commissions made up of delegates drawn from across the political spectrum set to work, one to redraft the 1945 constitution, the second to draft an entirely new constitution, and the third to draw up a legal framework for the transition and guidelines for the political parties. The commission drafting the new constitution, which was endorsed by the majority of the political parties, aimed to extend democratic participation, strengthen presidential authority and minimise the threat of conflict between the Congress and the executive. Where the 1945 constitution perpetuated the domination of the elite by limiting the franchise to literates who had registered to vote, the new constitution enfranchised illiterates. To ensure that the president was supported by a majority, the new constitution provided for a run-off between the two leading contenders in the event that no-one emerged as clear winner in the first round of voting. The president, who serves a four year term, must belong to a political party and cannot be re-elected. A single-chamber Congress was established, with 12 nationally-elected deputies sitting alongside 57 representatives elected at provincial level. The president's powers were increased to give him the right to appoint his own cabinet, to veto congressional proposals and to call a plebiscite in the event of congressional obstruction of his programme.

After nearly a year's delay (officially attributed to problems in drawing up the electoral register), a referendum took place in January 1978 to choose between the constitutions. In spite of a last-ditch campaign for a spoiled ballot led by León Febres Cordero, 90 per cent of the electorate turned out and 45 per cent voted for the new constitution. With everything now in place for the presidential elections due in July, the military began a cynical manipulation of the electoral law to exclude the candidates they disliked and to boost the chances of their favourite, Sixto Durán Ballén, a former mayor of Quito. In a move designed to bar Asaad Bucaram of the CFP from standing, the junta decreed that the new constitution would come into force only after the election; the old rules required the candidate's parents to be Ecuadorean-born, whereas the new rules would have allowed Bucaram to stand although his parents, of Lebanese origin, were naturalised citizens. Subsequent amendments to the electoral laws tried to reduce the field still further by requiring all candidates to have an academic degree, disqualifying Bucaram's wife from running for mayor of Guayaquil. Others ruled that ex-Presidents Velasco Ibarra and Carlos Arosemena were ineligible, and blocked the Liberal candidate, Francisco Huerta, on the grounds that his company had been awarded a government contract.

Once the election campaign was under way, the military became concerned that Bucaram might achieve power by a back door route, especially when the replacement CFP candidate, Jaime Roldós, headed the first round of the poll. A personable and charismatic young Guayaquil lawyer, Roldós was Bucaram's son-in-law, and at first appeared to be the puppet of the CFP leadership. The military's chief fear was that after they had returned to the barracks the civilian politicians would instigate investigations into charges of corruption and human rights infringements during the years of military rule; Roldós himself was campaigning under the slogan 'We will not forgive, we will not forget'. To safeguard their interests, the junta issued another decree requiring the new President to appoint the highest-ranking officer as Minister of Defence. This was a clear signal to Roldós that the armed forces would tolerate no interference in their affairs and countenance no investigation into their conduct while in power.

The transition to democracy now faced its most serious threat as right-wing civilians and their sympathisers inside the military manoeuvred to subvert the popular will. The second round of the election, which was legally required to be held within 45 days of the first, was delayed on the grounds that time had to be allowed for charges of electoral fraud to be investigated. The tribunal, *Tribunal Supremo Electoral* (TSE), supervising the election annulled around 100,000 votes, three quarters of them for Roldós and his running mate, Osvaldo Hurtado, though without affecting the overall result. It also withheld official recognition from the *Democracia Popular* (DP), the CFP's coalition partner and a vital element in Roldós' hopes of winning votes in the highlands. The 45 days between the first and second rounds of voting turned into nine months of procrastination, during which the Right orchestrated a smear campaign against the alleged Marxist inclinations of their opponents, and rumours of an impending coup swept the country. The army commander, Durán, and the Interior Minister, Jarrín, were both known to be opposed to the movement towards democracy. Suspicions that they were deliberately fostering a climate of chaos seemed to be substantiated when one of the presidential candidates, Abdón Calderón of the *Frente Radical Alfarista* (FRA), was assassinated in circumstances that appeared to implicate high-ranking officers (Jarrín was later gaoled for his involvement in the affair). All these events fuelled the uncertainty surrounding the forthcoming run-off.

The second round was nevertheless held (April 1979) and Jaime Roldós emerged as the clear winner with 68.5 per cent of the vote. The Roldós-Hurtado ticket carried all but one of the country's 20 provinces and polled nearly as well in the conservative highlands as in the CFP stronghold on the coast. The elections held simultaneously for the Congress seemed to provide further confirmation of the ascendency of the coalition led by the CFP, and the political eclipse of the Right. The armed forces' manipulation of the transition had failed to ensure the election of a candidate to their liking. The Right seemed to be discredited and in disarray.

New Forces or Old Politics?

By 1979 the smell of corruption, incompetence and political terrorism which hung over military rule meant that few Ecuadoreans lamented its passing. As the new, elected, government took office, it seemed that there were grounds for optimism that Ecuador's political development was about to catch up with the economic and social changes that had occurred in the 1970s. The continuing high petroleum revenues were available to finance a programme of social and economic reform. Roldós, at 38, Latin America's youngest-ever democratically-elected President, and his equally youthful running

Roldós' campaign poster, 'against oppression and poverty — the force of change — Roldós, the people's president', 1979.

45

mate and Vice-President, Osvaldo Hurtado, had received an unequivocal mandate for change. Under the slogan 'the force of change', their campaign projected the image of young, dynamic and intelligent politicians who embodied a new political force. Styling himself 'president of the poor' Roldós appealed to the peasant and working class majority who had failed to benefit from the oil boom, and to the *voto nuevo* – the young voters who had reached the qualifying age after the last open elections in 1968 and were participating in the democratic process for the first time.

Further evidence that the political mould had been broken seemed to come from the congressional elections held simultaneously with the second round of the presidential election. Here too, the returns seemed to confirm the eclipse of the traditional and populist parties: the three parties most closely identified with the old order – the Conservatives, the Liberals and the Social Christians – polled only 7.8 per cent, 8 per cent and 7 per cent respectively, and won only 17 seats out of 69. The *personalismo* parties – the Velasquistas, the CID and the PNR – fared even worse and won only six seats between them. The CFP also benefited from its association with the figure of Roldós, winning nearly a third of the vote and 29 seats. The reformist *Izquierda Democrática* (ID), led by another young and ambitious lawyer, Rodrigo Borja, followed with 18.4 per cent of the vote and 15 seats. The old pattern of voting on regional lines and according to regional loyalties seemed to be breaking down. Roldós defeated Durán in his Quito stronghold by a comfortable two to one margin, and the CFP established itself as a national party, capable of winning seats in the highlands and the *Oriente* as well as on the coast.

On closer inspection, however, optimism about the new political order turned out to be less well-founded. Regional divisions had not been eliminated but only disguised by the pairing of a *costeño* (coastal dweller) and a *serrano* (highlander) on the Roldós-Hurtado ticket. Ironically, by disqualifying Bucaram, the military forced the CFP to select a candidate with a much broader national appeal than its populist party boss. Many middle-class voters who would not have dreamed of voting for Bucaram saw Roldós as an efficient, reliable, technocratic reformer.

Unfortunately for Roldós, his sweeping second round majority was not mirrored in the composition of the new Congress, where even his own party, the CFP, was not committed to supporting his legislative programme. By the time of his inauguration on 10 August 1979, the new President already faced an opposition majority in Congress, orchestrated by none other than his former sponsor, Asaad Bucaram. Disagreements between the two leaders had surfaced during the election campaign when the CFP party boss objected to Roldós' choice of Hurtado, a long-time critic of Bucaram (Hurtado once described him as 'a loquacious and histrionic legislator who few people could take seriously') as his running mate, and the electoral alliance with Hurtado's DP. Deprived of the presidency, Bucaram was determined to run the country from his power base in the Congress. To do this he forged an unholy alliance between the CFP and its traditional enemy, the conservatives. The working majority thus created elected Bucaram to the presidency of the Congress, and he set about undermining the government's legislative programme.

Because of these deals struck in the Congress, and with Hurtado's DP still waiting for legal recognition as a party, Roldós found himself without any organised political support for his policies. Instead of enjoying a 'honeymoon' period, the new administration found itself immediately forced onto the defensive and compelled to devote its energies to constructing a political majority rather than pursuing its economic and social objectives. The President's only way out of the impasse was to resort to a time-honoured ploy and form a new party recruited from dissident *cefepistas* (members of the CFP) who disapproved of Bucaram's tactics and associates. Roldós' predicament was a tribute to the ingenuity of the old style politicians, but it also underlined the failure of the Law of Parties to establish an effective legal framework for the operation of political parties in the new system. The intention of the law had been to discourage the atomisation of parties into personality-led factions by requiring them to meet certain conditions before they could be licenced by the TSE. All candidates for public office had to belong to a legally recognised party. In practice, when ambitious politicians founded or joined a party, they did so in a spirit of opportunism rather than out of ideological commitment, and often showed little interest in building up a party organisation as distinct from a personal following. The absence of disciplined party loyalty quickly led to fragmentation and desertions. Hopes that the restructured democracy would provide strong and stable government evaporated as Ecuadorean politics reverted to their traditional character of the clash of personalities and executive-legislative conflict.

The *'Pugna de Poderes'**

The personal rivalry between Roldós and Bucaram turned into a debilitating and bitter battle between the two main branches of

*The power struggle.

government. Bucaram accused the President of betraying his party by ignoring the claims of some CFP militants when he appointed his first cabinet. The CFP leader called for the dismissal of municipal and provincial officials appointed by the previous military government and – in a move designed to thwart the formation of a pro-Roldós bloc in the Congress – urged the disqualification of any representative who switched party affiliation. Deploying his influence as President of the Congress, Bucaram was able to place his cronies and clients in all the key legislative and legal committees and ensure that they had an anti-executive majority.

On the economic front Bucaram began to outbid the government with populist proposals clearly designed to shipwreck the President's strategy. He started with a demand for a 20 per cent revaluation of the already overvalued *sucre*, arguing that it would cut the cost of living for the average Ecuadorean and reduce debt repayments. Next, the Congress approved bills setting the minimum monthly wage at 4,000 *sucres* (1,000 more than Roldós' proposal and double the previous minimum) and guaranteeing further increases tied to the cost of living index. Other measures calculated to embarrass the government included the reduction of the working week from 44 to 40 hours, retirement for women after 25 years of work, the expansion of higher and vocational education and a price freeze on basic goods, services and rents. These initiatives forced the President to veto or defer bills which, in the short term at least, would benefit his own supporters but which would soon set off inflationary pressures and incur unmanageable budget deficits. Bucaram seemed to be outflanking the 'president of the poor' and posing as the real spokesman and defender of the masses.

As rumours circulated that the military might be preparing to intervene again, Roldós pondered his political options. He could either call a plebiscite to approve the dissolution of Congress and the holding of fresh elections, gambling on the result; or he could try and construct a pro-government majority based on the second largest party, Rodrigo Borja's *Izquierda Democrática* (ID). He chose the latter option, and by early December 1979 a shaky coalition of the ID, Hurtado's DP and pro-Roldós *cefepistas* emerged. Predictably the new grouping proved to be inherently unstable. Some members of the ID, Borja amongst them, feared that too close identification with the government would damage the party's future electoral prospects, while others, led by Raúl Baca, argued that the political stalemate threatened the very existence of democracy. Roldós' CFP supporters resented the threat to their monopoly of bureaucratic posts posed by the ID's insistence on nominating its own cabinet ministers.

The new correlation of forces in the Congress did not guarantee a ceasefire between the two branches of government. The opposition were able to delay the centrepiece of Roldós' economic strategy, the VI Development Plan, covering the 1980-84 period. This had been drawn up by the National Development Council (*Consejo Nacional de Desarrollo*, CONADE) under the chairmanship of Hurtado, and contained impressive proposals for stimulating economic growth, tackling poverty and consolidating democracy by encouraging mass participation. The Plan focused on three main areas: rural development combining agrarian reform with increased agricultural output; improvements in social welfare provision, especially health, housing and education; and state investment of oil revenues into industrial and infrastructure development. Fourteen million dollars from both private and public sources were to be earmarked for investment in order to achieve an annual growth in GDP of 6.5 per cent, generate half a million jobs and reduce unemployment.

The Plan depended heavily on the goodwill of the private sector which was expected to provide more than 60 per cent of the proposed investment. Rather ominously, its viability hinged on the cooperation of domestic business interests and on the stability of the world oil market. Rather like the military government which had preceded him, Roldós hoped to develop a working relationship with the more progressive sectors of the business community, and to this end his cabinet appointments were calculated to reassure private enterprise that it had nothing to fear. The Finance Minister, Francisco Aspiazu, a banker from a prominent coastal family, and the Minister of Government, Roberto Dunn, a Guayaquil entrepreneur, were both well-known figures in financial circles. However, important members of the business elite, whose spokesman was León Febres Cordero, remained unimpressed by the government's plans and viewed Hurtado's 'communitarian' philosophy with deep suspicion. In particular they objected to labour and wage bills which they claimed were 'fiscally irresponsible', and to references to worker participation in enterprises. On the other side, the Left criticised the Plan for paying too little attention to income redistribution, agrarian reform and the expansion of the state sector.

The return to democracy coincided with unprecedentedly favourable economic circumstances for Ecuador. The Iranian revolution and the outbreak of the Gulf War triggered a second oil boom in which prices tripled during 1979-80. Ecuadorean crude which had sold at just over 13 dollars a barrel in 1976 now commanded prices at around 35 dollars a barrel. During 1979, oil export earnings leaped by 85 per cent over the previous year, to more than a billion dollars. In

1980 they rose by a further 35 per cent. This windfall made it possible for the government to finance wage increases and promote industrialisation through state protectionism and the provision of incentives. On the other hand, there were foreseeable constraints on revenue in the shape of high levels of domestic oil consumption (growing at 10-15 per cent annually) and the virtual standstill in exploration and development activity. The urgency of this problem was highlighted by the World Bank's refusal to grant loans to Ecuador until a more 'realistic' pricing policy was adopted, i.e. one of restraining domestic consumption in favour of increased exports. The government approached the issue with understandable reluctance as previous attempts to push up petrol prices at the pump had provoked rioting and disorder. This measure would have meant increasing popular transport fares, hitting hardest at the government's own supporters. Eventually the government's hand was forced by the prospect that, if present trends continued, Ecuador would soon become a net importer of oil, coupled with a worsening liquidity crisis. After a modest price rise in January, Roldós authorised a three-fold increase in the domestic price of petroleum products. Fortunately for the government (and perhaps not entirely by accident), these coincided with a war scare over the disputed frontier with Peru, and as a result the anticipated protests were comparatively muted by the groundswell of patriotic and nationalist fervour which swept the country.

The Professor as President

With his government still hamstrung by the blocking and delaying tactics of Bucaram and the opposition, Roldós looked for a new way to break the impasse. When the Congress opened a new line of attack by starting impeachment proceedings against Interior Minister Carlos Feraud in April 1980, Roldós' supporters drafted a constitutional amendment to enable him to take up the option of holding a plebiscite on new parliamentary elections. Again the President shrank from mobilising mass opinion, and chose instead a compromise worked out by a Commission of Notables made up of political, business and religious leaders. For a brief moment the political horizon seemed to clear: Raúl Baca's election as the new leader of Congress seemed to promise less obstruction and more cooperation; the President could now count on his own political party, *Pueblo, Cambio, Democracia* (PCD), founded by 12 defecting *cefepistas*; and the December 1980 local elections delivered a sharp rebuff to Bucaram's CFP (whose vote collapsed to less than eight per cent) and registered a continuing erosion of the Right. But before any advantage could be gained from the consolidation of a reformist centre – the *convergencia democrática* – Roldós, his wife and the Defence Minister, were killed in an aircrash in the southern province of Loja near the Peruvian border. Although Vice-President Hurtado immediately assumed office as the constitution provided, and pledged himself to continue the policies of his predecessor, he soon dashed hopes that he would be more aggressive in pursuit of economic and social reform, stressing instead the need for austerity and economic responsibility.

Hurtado inherited from Roldós uneasy relations with the Congress. To these were added the onset of a new economic crisis and trade union militancy on a scale and intensity hitherto unknown in Ecuador. Under the pressure of such forces, the reformist centre that had seemed to be taking shape quickly began to disintegrate again. The *convergencia democrática* only lasted a matter of weeks and was undermined when the ID broke ranks to join in a censure of the Minister of Government. Once again Congress and the executive became locked in a fierce battle over spending plans, and parliamentary time was taken up with calling ministers to account for their policies and actions. Austerity was an unpopular refrain after the brief boom of the last few years and could hardly be expected to rally support for Hurtado, who now found himself assailed from all sides.

During 1982 Ecuador experienced its first major economic crisis since the start of the oil era. In this year oil revenues fell by around 11 per cent and the value of exports by eight per cent. Hurtado tried to make up some of the shortfall by imposing higher taxes on the rich, prosecuting tax evaders and rigorously applying corporate taxes. Predictably these measures met with a hostile reception from the business and commercial communities who were anyway highly suspicious of Hurtado's motives. In August 1981 the government charged 700 firms with tax fraud and introduced legislation to prevent companies from declaring themselves bankrupt in order to dismiss workers. The President of the Guayaquil Chamber of Industries – the employers' federation – already stung by congressional proposals for consumer defence and worker democracy laws, claimed that they were victims of 'a socialist plot' to destroy private enterprise.

The growing burden of foreign debt servicing also forced Ecuador to look for ways of renegotiating and rescheduling repayments. This meant accepting an IMF (International Monetary Fund) approved stabilisation programme as a condition of rescheduling. In May Hurtado devalued the *sucre*, for the first time in ten years, by 32 per cent. At the same time he imposed new tariffs on imports, cut

51

subsidies on fuel and basic foodstuffs, and postponed major development projects. By early 1983 it was becoming clear that these measures would be inadequate to deal with the crisis. This was compounded by natural disaster, when the unpredictable offshore El Niño current caused widespread floods in the coastal provinces, disrupting agricultural production, reducing output by up to one third, wrecking bridges and roads, and fuelling inflation as shortages forced up food prices. Once again the government had to go cap in hand to the IMF. It had to introduce a stabilisation package as the price of assistance. The *sucre* was devalued by a further 27.2 per cent – it had now fallen by half against the dollar in less than a year – and this was accompanied by a surcharge on imports, and a programme of mini-devaluations which were soon running at an annual rate in excess of 40 per cent.

Parallel adjustments took place in oil policy. In July 1982 Ecuador became the first OPEC member to announce an official price cut of 1.75 dollars a barrel. Production was also lowered to just over 200,000 barrels per day following marketing difficulties during which a large surplus of unsold oil had accumulated. CEPE was authorised to sell wherever it could find a market – this effectively sanctioned further price reductions. The Hydrocarbons Law was modified to attract foreign investors and eleven new exploration blocks were offered on undemanding contract terms for 1983. The search for new sources of oil was becoming an urgent priority given that oil output was predicted to peak around the middle of the 1980s and then decline. CEPE's soaring debts and crippling repayments sharply reduced its effectivenesss in carrying on exploration activities and inevitably gave the foreign companies a stronger hand in negotiations.

The stabilisation measures forced on a reluctant government signalled a lurch to the right. The emphasis now was on slashing public expenditure, reducing state subsidies and rescuing firms facing bankruptcy as their profits and turnovers dwindled. The sharp rise in prices – inflation topped 48 per cent in 1983 – alienated the trade unions as they saw how the poor were being made to carry the weight of the crisis. With few friends in the Congress and little or no influence within the centre-right cabinet, the labour movement resorted to the only political weapon at its disposal; street protest and the general strike. Although a general strike occurred during Roldós' presidency, the most combative and effective of the strikes were held in September and October 1982 when the government was forced to declare a state of emergency.

Although the frequency of strike action reflected a growing militancy and an ability to mobilise mass support on occasion, the goal

52

of labour unity still proved elusive. Protests too often degenerated into tactical and political squabbles among the confederations and independent unions, splitting moderates from militants over issues like the duration of the strike, the precise objectives, and whether to maintain dialogue with the government or take up a position of intransigence. The trade unions' inability to sustain a prolonged strike and maintain solidarity for longer than a token 24 or 48 hours meant that strikes were symbolic rather than effective. It was comparatively easy for the employers, holding all the cards of a great reserve of work-hungry unemployed, to force poorly-led and poorly-paid workers back to work once the initial enthusiasm for the strike wore thin.

For its part, the government, while critical of disruptive action, always declared itself willing to enter into negotiations with the strikers in order to reach a compromise. Ministers stressed the common interest both sides had in the preservation of democracy which, given the ever-present threat of military intervention, inclined many union leaders to pragmatism. They could also point to real achievements in the government's record in reversing the dictatorship's anti-labour legislation, and to the four minimum wage increases amounting to 330 per cent over the last five years. Wages were now reviewed biannually instead of annually by more than a hundred commissions comprising government, labour and employer representatives. In addition, the Ministry of Labour had helped to put union finances on a firmer footing by authorising deductions from members' wages, and ensured that redundant workers received dismissal payments. Certainly the democratic environment had encouraged the growth of the labour movement: 1,000 new *sindicatos* (unions) were formed in the four years after 1979 and by 1983 the unions had a total of 446,956 members. But all these claims, however true, cut little ice with the hundreds of thousands of workers in non-unionised activities, or the millions of semi- or un-employed, or families trying to make ends meet on the small incomes of too few wage-earners.

The economic crisis and the political manoeuverings in the run-up to the 1984 elections left the embattled President isolated. The major political parties were reluctant to be associated with Hurtado's unpopular policies in the run-up to the poll, and the dissolution of the reformist centre proceeded apace. When Hurtado made some injudicious remarks about the late President's choice of ministers, his Vice-President – Roldós' younger brother – countered by accusing him of abandoning his brother's policies and giving priority to debt repayments when he should have been tackling pressing social and economic problems. The President asserted his authority by excluding Roldós from cabinet meetings, at which point the PCD withdrew from the governing coalition. Hurtado's attempt to reconstitute a majority by bringing CFP ministers into the government was defeated by Asaad Bucaram's son and political heir, Averroes Bucaram, who took the CFP back into opposition, leaving the President only with his own DP and some independents.

This shifting and unstable political scene underlined the failure of attempts to reform party politics in Ecuador. *Personalismo* continued to predominate over policies and issues, and the proliferation of parties as the private following of would-be power brokers continued unabated. The factionalism of politics on the coast, in particular, was illustrated by the formation in January 1983 by Abdalá Bucaram (the late President's brother-in-law and another of the vast political network of Bucaram interests) of a personal vehicle, the *Partido Roldocista Ecuatoriano*, whose philosophy, programme and constituency quite clearly overlapped with that of the PCD. It provided further evidence, if any were needed, that personality and *caudillismo* were the most potent forces in Ecuadorean politics. Finally, constitutional changes in 1983, which scheduled congressional, municipal and presidential elections together, seemed certain to benefit smaller parties and guaranteed an even more fragmented Congress. It was hardly a surprise when nine candidates declared for the presidency in 1984 and 17 parties – the largest number ever in Ecuador's democratic history – contested the congressional elections.

The 1984 Elections

That the elections took place at all owed much to the determination of Osvaldo Hurtado who, unable to stand for re-election himself, pushed through unpopular measures that a campaigning president might have avoided. Past economic crises had often been the prelude to military intervention, but Hurtado weathered a storm of criticism and contemptuously dismissed civilian attempts to engineer a coup. In spite of his difficulties Hurtado emphasised that his main achievement was the consolidation of the democratic system. However, the persistence of *personalismo* politics meant that most voters were still being denied a meaningful choice between political parties offering distinct ideological and policy platforms. The highly factionalised state of politics ensured that politicians' energies would continue to be absorbed in building up and holding together unstable and transitory coalitions.

54

'Hurtado, Borja and León, don't pay the debt by sacrificing the people. Don't pay the foreign debt'. Demonstration during the 1984 elections.

At the start of the 1984 election campaign, it looked as if the reformist centre held the winning hand and ought to romp home. Roldós' victory five years earlier on a social democratic platform coupled with the progress made by the ID seemed to reinforce this probability. The traditional Right, undermined by the social and economic changes that had occurred in the 1970s and badly beaten in 1979, appeared to be in permanent and irreversible decline while the Left showed few signs of overcoming its electoral weakness and attachment to ideological factionalism. The reformist centre candidate, Rodrigo Borja of the ID, led the poll in the first round of the elections (January 1984), pushing the standard-bearer of the Right, León Febres Cordero, comfortably into second place and assuming the mantle of heir-apparent as the run-off began. Borja was confident that he would inherit the bulk of the centre-left vote which had originally divided up among eight candidates, but his optimistic reading of the electoral arithmetic took for granted that the 'reformist centre' actually existed and had a political majority, and that the party leaders with whom he made deals could deliver their supporters' votes to him. In reality, the atomised parties of the centre and left were reluctant to endorse Borja when the second round of the election got under way, and two populist parties, the CFP and the FRA, followed

León Febres Cordero during an election rally, 1984.

Julio Etchart

their regionalist instincts – as well as the economic interests they represented – and worked openly for Febres Cordero, the local candidate of the coast. The divisions in the Borja camp were in sharp contrast to the unity of the Right, which had been noticeably absent in 1979. Following that defeat, which had given them a sharp fright, Sixto Durán had emphasised the need for agreement on a single candidate; with the formation of the *Frente de Reconstrucción Nacional* (FRN), Febres – who as we have seen had been very much at the forefront as a critic of the Roldós and Hurtado administrations, and whose conservative credentials were impeccable – claimed the undisputed leadership of the Right, and the huge financial and media resources that that entailed.

In spite of these obvious advantages Febres had only managed second place in the first round of the voting. The results of the congressional elections brought little consolation, either; the Right took just 16 seats as against the combined total of 33 for centre and left parties. Stung by this setback, the FRN blamed electoral fraud and malpractice, claiming rather disingenuously that the disqualification of some votes in Guayaquil had cost their candidate first place. Febres subsequently revamped his campaign strategy and, enlisting the assistance of a Colombian public relations firm, adopted a new slogan, 'Food, Shelter and Jobs'. He skilfully exploited the traditional patterns of Ecuadorean political habits: a populist programme, with a plan for low cost housing, which appealed to the poor; the cultivation of regionalist sentiment, which on the coast was heightened by the feeling that the advent of the oil boom had shifted the country's centre of gravity to Quito at Guayaquil's expense; and the portrayal of his opponent as a dangerous, unprincipled and unpatriotic left-winger manipulated by external forces, an atheist smeared with the brush of his association with Hurtado's unpopular administration. By shifting the focus of the campaign firmly away from programmes and towards personalities (virtually no policy debates took place), Febres could play up his macho image as a 'tough guy' and appeal to the populist and *caudillist* legacy of Velasco Ibarra and Asaad Bucaram. To emphasise the point he arrived at political meetings on horseback.

The style worked. A disconcerted Borja found himself out-manoeuvred as Febres, in spite of finishing second in 15 of the Republic's 20 provinces, won landslide victories in Guayas (which alone contained 25 per cent of the electorate), Manabí and Los Ríos. As a result, Ecuador once again found itself with a chief executive squaring up to a hostile opposition majority in the Congress.

4. The Forgotten Majority

In the mid-1980s, Ecuador could look back on more than a decade of military or civilian governments which claimed an explicit commitment to economic growth, development and modernisation, which promised to work for social justice and respond to the long-postponed needs of the poor, and which were underpinned to a lesser or greater extent by the fabulous and unprecedented inflow of oil wealth. A quick overview of Ecuadorean society as Hurtado's government came to an end and Febres Cordero prepared to assume the presidency shows, however, that as far as the conditions of life for vast masses of Ecuadoreans were concerned, the years of 'development' and 'social justice' had achieved very little.

The evidence of detailed studies of social conditions which have been made by a group of Dutch and Latin American social scientists from the Institute of Social Studies at The Hague, makes it clear that the majority of Ecuadoreans still have lives of grim desperation inconsistent with the country's actual and potential wealth. In spite of the supposedly dynamising effect of the oil boom, the bottom 40 per cent of the Ecuadorean population received around 5.2 per cent of total income, while the top 20 per cent took around 72 per cent; 54.5 per cent of the population – approximately five million people – were officially classified as living below the poverty threshhold.

Informal Employment

In 1975 just over half (51.2 per cent) of the workforce were engaged in what specialists in development studies have called 'informal sector employment'. Wrapped in this technical terminology are conditions of work which are almost unimaginable for the inhabitants of the affluent welfare societies of the First World. The more than a million

Ecuadoreans trapped in this pattern of labour are, characteristically, without any real definition of their work and without any real security of employment. They may be sacked from their job at any time, at the whim of the employer and without any reason being given; there is no minimum wage for their employment, they have to negotiate a 'fair wage' with an employer who holds all the cards in his hand; there is no provision for accident or injury while employed, nor pension for long-term disability incurred in the course of employment; there is no insurance scheme to ensure some kind of income, wage or family supplement, however small, during periods of unemployment or between employment; there are no health or safety regulations controlling the conditions under which they work, nor anything regulating the total number of hours in each shift. In short, 'informal sector employment' is a euphemism for the most savage face of Third World capitalism, the extremes of exploitation for those Ecuadoreans not lucky enough to have a 'regular job'.

Most typically the area of domestic, personal and household services includes 97.3 per cent of its workers in 'informal sector employment'. It is also widespread in woodworking products (84.4 per cent), agriculture (67.5 per cent), retail trade (64.8 per cent), and clothing and textiles (63.3 per cent). These activities are usually basic, unskilled work not requiring much in the way of qualifications, or even

A suburbio *in Guayaquil.*

literacy, and they are often the first destination of migrants from the countryside or new young entrants into the labour force.

It is notable, though not perhaps surprising, that the economic sectors in which informal employment patterns are most widespread are often those in which a large number of the workers are women. The employment structure systematically discriminates against women, who make up around a third of the total workforce. The average wage for female workers is barely half (54.6 per cent) the average wage for male workers. Small wonder that in recent years women have come to be amongst the most active and militant members of the popular classes in demanding change and improvement in their status.

In 1974, 34.9 per cent of the workforce were unemployed or underemployed; by 1982 this situation was virtually unchanged, with 33.4 per cent under- or unemployed. It is clear that the mere fact of new wealth has made no real difference to the bottom third of the workforce, and that lack of work is a structural problem which needs structural solutions, not a technical problem which can be solved by 'quick fixes' within the existing socio-economic framework.

Housing

Like other Third World countries, Ecuador has experienced a growing migration in recent decades from the countryside to the towns as the rural population has tried to escape the problems of poverty and limited access to land, and find work and a better life. In 1962, 1,251,000 people (27.9 per cent of the population) lived in the towns and cities; by 1974, there were 2,299,000 people (35.2 per cent of the population); and by 1986 51 per cent of the population lived in urban areas. The housing crisis is therefore most acute in the cities, where the flood of immigrants far outstrips the provision of urban services and facilities. In Guayaquil, for example (which receives more immigrants than any other Ecuadorean city, and where the problems are therefore most acute), in the four years from 1978 to 1982, the population of the *suburbio* (squatter settlement) of Mapasingue, northwest of the city centre, increased more than tenfold, from 9,800 people to 100,000. To the south of the city centre, in the unhealthy, low-lying semi-swampland of the *suburbio* of El Guasmo, the population increased almost twenty-fivefold, from 8,000 to 200,000 people. In these marginal areas, it has been estimated that around 75-80 per cent of the population have incomes below the official minimum wage.

So what are housing conditions like in the *suburbios* that sprawl

60

around the periphery of a city such as Guayaquil? A major problem is that many houses are built on or below the level of the surrounding tidal rivers, and are vulnerable to the effects of heavy rainfall and the rivers rising. An urgent need in these areas is *relleno*, the uplevelling of the land with all kinds of materials – garbage, gravel, sand – to raise the houses and roads above the floodwater level. Where the roads are not yet raised the necessary two or three metres, houses are often connected to each other by walkways or bridges on piles. The inhabitants of the settlements are liable at any moment to be cut off from access to the rest of the city (and their employment), and cannot be reached by the public transportation and water supply tank trucks on which they depend for fresh water. The houses themselves in these areas are usually crude constructions with bamboo walls, wooden floors and zinc sheet roofs. Such constructions give inadequate protection against dampness, humidity and mosquitoes; there is an ever-present danger of fire; and they are almost impossible to make secure against thieves and burglars. Overcrowding and lack of privacy is acute; around 72 per cent of dwellings exceed the maximum acceptable density of two people to a room, and families of up to ten people living in a single room are common. Piped water supply and sewerage are effectively non-existent; 89.3 per cent of houses lack the former and 85.7 per cent the latter. Most people either have outdoor latrines or simply discharge their body wastes directly into the rivers and streams.

The *suburbios* are of course around the periphery of the cities. The housing crisis also extends into the city centres, however, in the form of the *tugurios*. These old houses formerly belonged to the upper classes who have since departed to the fashionable new North American-style suburbs outside the city. The large decaying properties left behind are rented out in apartments or individual rooms, and here living conditions are bad and population densities high. In Guayaquil, the most recent studies show that more than half a million people are located in the *suburbios* around the periphery and more than a quarter of a million in the *tugurios* of the city centre. At the most conservative estimate, this is about 60 per cent of the city's population and some estimates are as high as 80 per cent. The inrush of migrants has been very profitable for property speculators who have bought up old houses in the centre and fractionalised them into multitudes of tiny apartments which can be let at high rents; and for landowners and land speculators who have seen their worthless lands on the fringes of the city subjected to invasions by squatters who are anxious to legalise their occupation and escape the threat of eviction by paying for their plots.

In the countryside, overcrowding is slightly less severe than in the towns (though at 50 per cent of dwellings overcrowded it is still a problem). But lack of basic services is more acute than in the towns. In 1982, 41.9 per cent of houses were classified as non-permanent, 84.5 per cent had no piped water or toilet facilities and 94.5 per cent had no sewerage.

Health and Nutrition

Health provision generally for Ecuadoreans is poor. Medical facilities and resources for the health sector as a whole are oriented towards curative-based activities and the urban areas, rather than towards preventive medicine and the improvement of the basic determinants of health (nutrition, drinking water, sanitation). Because of this, public subsidies and health programmes tend to benefit the better-off urban dwellers rather than the poor, who remain a prey to parasitic, infectious and diarrhoeal diseases. In 1978 more than 45,000 women – a third of all those having their baby in a hospital – suffered complications with pregnancy, delivery or puerpery. More than 33,000 people were admitted to hospital suffering from the results of accidents or acts of violence, more than 17,000 from enteritis and other diarrhoeal diseases, more than 17,000 from respirational diseases, more than 6,000 from typhus, paratyphus and diphtheria. These statistics are based on hospital reports and are therefore skewed in favour of the relatively better-off social classes who can afford medical treatment. Public health care facilities in theory do not charge for medical consultancies, and newly-qualified doctors have to serve an obligatory year in the public medical service before they can start a private practice. In practice, there is a low ratio of public beds and doctors to population in the poorer districts. Hospital pharmacies which are supposed to supply medicines at cost-price often do not have them so that patients must obtain them from high-priced private pharmacies. Hospitals and health centres are often situated too far away from patients to be reasonably accessible, emergency attendance and ambulance services are almost non-existent, and low morale and absenteeism amongst medical personnel are widespread. The real figures of health demands are much higher than the hospital figures and embrace large numbers of people who go no further than medical first-aid posts, or resort to folk healers (*curanderos* who include magical techniques in their treatments, and *hierbateros* who use folk remedies based on natural products) or engage in self-medication.

The group most at risk from poor health and nutritional standards is, predictably, children. In 1985 the death rate for infants in the first twelve months of life was 67 per thousand; a further 13.4 per thousand died before their fourth birthday. In 1980-81 a survey in one of the Guayaquil *suburbios* revealed that one in five children was suffering at any one time from diarrhoea. The high infant and child mortality and morbidity are concentrated in the bottom third of income earners and are usually caused by preventable diseases and malnutrition.

While it is the case that Ecuador is not faced with the problems of endemic hunger which afflict the countries of Africa or South East Asia, it does suffer from a chronic condition of malnutrition which restricts the full physical and mental development of the population. Measurements of nutrition based on United Nations norms for minimal healthy diet established in the 1970s show that malnutrition is a serious problem for around 57 per cent of the population. FAO norms specify around 2,300 calories per person per day as the minimum intake; the average intake in Ecuador is around 2,050-2,100 calories, a shortfall of about 11 per cent. Protein intakes are marginally less deficient in quantity, but are mainly of vegetable origin and are heavily deficient in animal proteins (between 15 and 24 per cent). In the *suburbios* even the most basic element for the maintenance of life – drinking water – is a scarce commodity. There is seldom a piped water supply and people are normally dependent on the supply brought in by tank trucks, which is often irregular, is relatively expensive to buy – it accounted for around one-fifth of the minimum family income in the early 1980s – and then is not always safe to drink.

The figures for diet deficiency are alarming enough in themselves when one considers the effects of a lifetime's nutritional deficit on physical and mental development. They become even more frightening when we consider that – like other indices of deprivation – they are disproportionately concentrated into children, women and the poor. Because of cultural conditioning or lack of education, many families do not accept that young children and pregnant or nursing mothers have special nutritional needs. In consequence, around 67 per cent of infants (up to five years of age) and around 18 per cent of pregnant or nursing women have been classified as suffering from malnourishment. At the same time, sheer economic need has dictated that the adult male or males in the family should receive a larger share and better quality of the family's food supply because, traditionally, nutrition has been associated with the capacity to earn by working. The short-term need to ensure the family's immediate survival has meant that the long-term future of masses of poor families – their children – has had to be sacrificed.

63

Education

The formal education system in Ecuador consists of six years of primary education, which in theory is obligatory for all children from the age of six. This may be followed by six years of secondary school to obtain the basic high-school diploma, the *bachillerato* which in theory is the passport to a decently-paid job or into higher education (another five years' study). In practice, almost half (47.5 per cent in 1982) of those children who enrol in primary school fail to complete the first cycle of education and qualify for entry into secondary education; most drop out in the second or third year. More than half (53.1 per cent in 1982) of the children who enrol in secondary school fail to complete the cycle and qualify for the *bachillerato*. The reasons for these high drop-out rates are learning difficulties resulting from overcrowded homes and poor studying facilities, the expense of education (inability of many families to pay for school uniform, books, writing implements, etc), the pressures on children once they reach the age of 12-14 to go out and work, and the effect of malnutrition on mental development and learning ability.

The high drop-out rate in primary school also means that the real levels of illiteracy are almost certainly higher than the officially claimed ones. According to official statistics, the adult illiteracy rate fell from 25 per cent in 1974 to 16.7 per cent in 1982. Other studies, however, suggest that people with three years or less of primary school are functionally illiterate; this means that the real illiteracy rate may well be nearer to 25 per cent. Again, educational deprivation is disproportionately concentrated among the urban and rural poor, where functional illiteracy rates are probably nearer to 40 per cent than to 25 or 16 per cent.

As Ecuador has evolved away from a predominantly peasant and agricultural society towards an urban and commercial one, education – even at the minimal level of being able to read and write – has become increasingly important for improving people's chances of entering the labour market and enabling them to secure the basic material and social decencies of life for themselves and their families. Studies have shown that there are close correlations between levels of education and levels of income. The illiterate and semi-literate are therefore effectively locked out of a future in Ecuador.

Popular Responses

It is obvious that the people who have mainly benefited from the years of 'development' and 'reform' are the middle and upper classes, professionals, businessmen and state employees. By contrast, there is a large population – persistently around 50 or 60 per cent, by almost whatever index of poverty or deprivation one uses to measure it – of the poor and indigent. This 'forgotten majority' has been largely passed by. They remain locked into a poverty trap of poor housing, poor diet, poor health, low education, and unemployment or underemployment. But in recent years the popular classes have been less and less willing to see themselves ignored without protest. Since the formal political system, whether military or civilian, has not delivered the goods to them, they are resorting more and more to other forms of mobilisation around social movements rather than political programmes. Some of the most effective of these new social forces are to be found amongst working-class women in the towns, and in the Indian federations in the countryside.

A good example of women's mobilisation is the *barrio* (neighbourhood) committee of the Indio Guayas district of Guayaquil, which has been studied in detail by the British sociologist Caroline Moser. This *barrio* is a typical low-income community where employment is usually in unskilled and non-unionised jobs in small-scale enterprises or irregular casual work in marginal service activities. While most households are male-headed, the predominant form of marital relationship is the *compromiso*, or free union, in which there is a high rate of desertion by the male partner. The motivation to invade the low-lying swampland is to own a home and escape the prohibitive rents charged nearer the city centre. Even so, many women are reluctant to make the move to Indio Guayas. The *barrio* is distant from the city centre, lacks water, sewerage and roads, there is a danger to children from the rickety system of catwalks over the swamp that unite the houses, and the burden of domestic labour under such primitive conditions is very heavy. There is also a considerable fear of loneliness. In such circumstances the women have developed strong mutual aid relationships with each other, formalising them through the institution of *comadrazgo* (godparenthood) on the birth of their children. The struggle for survival has forced them to create and retain friendships with their neighbours and this has led in turn to an increasing understanding of their situation and the need to try and do something about it. The well-known procedure by which self-help committees petition for services in exchange for votes has also been influential in promoting popular participation.

Barrio committees are not, of course, new in Ecuador. They began in the 1940s with the emergence of a political system in which populist parties bought votes by providing infrastructure and services. Until the 1960s such committees tended to be short-lived, coming into being just before elections and disbanding soon afterwards. However, the shockwaves from the Cuban revolution, the Alliance for Progress, and the growth of concern among liberals and development planners about the situation of the squatter settlements, gave such committees a more permanent character. The creation of a Department of Community Development by the Guayaquil Municipality and the announcement in 1972 of an ambitious plan to infill large areas of swampland, inspired the formation of hundreds of *barrio* committees. Although the years of military government and the cancellation of the infill project in 1976 for lack of funds (at the height of the oil boom) led to the collapse of many of them, the experience of local self-help organisations gained during these years was an important one for the inhabitants of the *suburbios*.

The *barrio* committee, Indio Guayas, was formed in 1975 from the efforts of some of the women. At first they did not see themselves as candidates for leadership. However, the ineptitude of their first president, a male white-collar worker who was deemed for that reason to be the most appropriate choice, led to his replacement a year later by Susana, who was still in office in the early 1980s. This experience is not at all unique. In the *suburbio* where Indio Guayas is located, only four of the *barrio* committees were headed by women in 1976; by 1982 this had doubled to eight. In fact, whether *barrio* committees have men or women as their elected officers, it is mainly the women who are responsible for their day-to-day work, organising and participating in meetings, demonstrations, protests at the municipality and canvassing. They are often accompanied on these occasions by their children, because of the lack of childminding facilities. The men are neither regular nor reliable in participating in these mobilisations, and often do so only as a result of considerable pressure from the women.

The run-up to the 1978 elections which followed the departure of the military government was the first opportunity for political mobilisation since the creation of the *barrio*. In response to approaches from political parties ranging from extreme right to extreme left, all anxious to co-opt the new *suburbio*, the 20-odd *barrio* committees formed a united front which finally decided to give their support to the *Izquierda Democrática* (ID). This decision was not based on any particular affinity with the party's centre-left ideological line but on a realistic appreciation of its capacity to deliver the promised services in exchange for votes. The front continued to give its support to the ID into the early 1980s and finally received the long-fought-for *relleno*, electricity and water supply.

The experience of mobilisation and working together has brought

66

all kinds of intangible but nevertheless important benefits to the women of the *barrio*. It has enabled many to increase their control over their own lives as they have gained confidence to question the subordinate status of women in Ecuadorean family culture. Those who have actively pursued educational opportunities and the economic independence that vocational skills can bring have also come to insist on being treated on a basis of equality and respect in their marital lives. Politically, it has increased their awareness and understanding of how the Ecuadorean political system works, where real power lies, how local government operates and how political parties function in the allocation of resources. They have seen the ways that corruption penetrates the decision-making process and how the poor are persistently manipulated for political ends. While they have become more cynical about the political system, they have also become more skilled in the techniques of making it work for them and for the poor in general rather than against them. For the leaders, at least, the cost has often been high; most working-class women presidents of *barrio* committees have seen their marriages break down in the face of conflict between them and their husbands over their political activities. But as Susana said in her case, 'If I am a leader and people have trust in me I cannot let them down ... I am not going to let [my husband] dominate me too much ... Once he sees that I don't obey him, he'll have to decide whether he wants to go on or go to the devil. What does marriage do for us? I have always worked since I was a young girl'.

During the last fifteen years, starting with the petrol boom, there has been an increased capacity for other popular sectors to mobilise. The growing industrial economy has given rise to increased union mobilisation, however, this mobilisation has been very worker-centred and has tended to marginalise the peasant sector (nearly 50 per cent of the population still live in the rural areas). The countryside has been the site of a prolonged struggle of resistance since the arrival of the Spaniards. At times this has been at the level of rebellion and general uprisings. In the *sierra*, the Indians have had their traditional forms of organisation for hundreds of years and although the form has been modified, the process of organisation is well established. The first national Indian federation (FEI) was formed in 1944 and the first coastal peasant organisation was formed in 1954. From the end of the 1950s the state began to assume an increasingly important role in the countryside, promulgating the first Agrarian Reform Law in 1964 and the second in 1973. During this time, two important national peasant organisations were formed – FENOC and ECUARUNARI (the latter mainly representing Indian organisations in the *sierra*). As FEI was

Ecuadorean Labour

Between 1970 and 1980 the percentage of the economically active population which is organised rose from 10 per cent to 18 per cent. Although numerically small, the union movement has a significant potential for industrial action and for leading opposition to government. The United Workers Front (FUT) has been functioning since 1975 and became a fully established organisation in 1980. It is formed by the three main union confederations, the CEOSL (Social Democrat), CEDOC (Socialist) and CTE (Communist) and represents 67 per cent of the unionised workforce (23 per cent are in independent unions and 10 per cent in three small confederations).

The independent unions account for certain key groups of workers, notably the petroleum workers, bus and taxi drivers, teachers and bank employees. Some of these unions, like the teachers and the sugar workers, have taken militant action in pursuit of economic demands, but poor organisation, internal divisions and the conservatism of some unions is an obstacle to political solidarity.

The FUT has called nine general strikes since 1975, and especially in 1982 and 1983 became the main negotiator for the popular sectors with the government. It is now coordinating certain actions with the UGTE (Maoist) and CEDOC-CLAT (Christian Democrat) union federations. There was a fall-off in organising capacity during the government of Febres Cordero, because of the anti-union policies which the government pursued and also because of the growing control by political parties, including those of the centre-left, who wish to see the unions' power reduced. One of the other limiting factors in the growth of the FUT has been the continuing divisions between the left-wing parties. Nevertheless, the FUT still represents an important mobilising capacity and will be a force to be reckoned with if it is capable of combining popular demands with the workers' demands.

unable to adapt to meet changing circumstances it has gradually lost power.

In part because of the growth of the agro-industrial model and its application in new zones such as the jungle, and in part because of their continued marginalisation, an important new area of ethnic organisation has grown up over the last fifteen years, represented by CONFENIAE (jungle and lowland Indians) and ECUARUNARI (*sierran* Indians). These two organisations have now formed a coordinating body CONAIE. Parallel with the movements towards unity in the unions, there has been a movement towards unity in the rural sectors with the formation of the *Coordinadora Campesina-Indigena* which groups FENOC, ECUARUNARI, FEI and various

Union demonstration, 1 May 1980.

69

independent groups and acts in coordination with CONFENIAE.

This coordinating body has approved a programme for struggle with six main points:

- to bring agrarian reform under peasant control.
- to abolish the Agricultural Development Law of 1979 (this law puts severe restrictions on the process of agrarian reform).
- to expel the religious sects and their respective 'development' institutions, which divide the peasant and Indian communities.
- to abolish the National Security Law and for an end to repression in the rural areas.
- to integrate the peasant organisations into the direction of the FUT.
- to demand respect for the land, cutoms, rights and language of the Indian peoples.

Additionally, the Indian organisations through CONAIE have called for various extra areas to be included in a wider platform of struggle. These are, bilingual education and literacy training for the Indian groups, under the control of their own organisations; development of traditional medicine; a degree of self-determination for the Indian peoples using as a basis their own traditional organisations.

In general, both the peasant and the Indian organisations have become increasingly active politically, and various new forms of organisation are beginning to emerge. In the coastal region, for example, there is a coordinated scheme for the commercialisation of four basic products (maize, soya, rice and cocoa) between five of the main provincial peasant federations, grouping in total some ten thousand small producers, organised principally in cooperatives and agricultural associations. In the *sierra* and jungle, there are two important projects for bilingual education (in the provinces of Bolívar and Napo), which apart from providing community-controlled bilingual education to some three thousand children in about sixty communities, have also established a training centre for Indian teachers in the production of appropriate teaching materials drawing on their own history, culture and knowledge.

All these schemes are under the direct control of popular organisations, and are a direct response to government neglect, or to government policies which favour the wealthy at the expense of the poor. The schemes incorporate political training for the base organisations and the second grade organisations starting from the political context of the actions being undertaken.

At a rough estimate, some 60 per cent of the rural population is organised at a local level, and some 50 per cent of these belong to one or other provincial peasant organisation.

A successful example of an Indian self-help movement is the Shuar

70

'We won't pay the landlords for our lands!' Ecuarunari.

Federation. The traditional Shuar homeland is a roughly triangular region bounded by the Pastaza river in the north, the Andes to the west, and the de facto Peruvian-Ecuadorean frontier to the south-east. There are two main groups, the Untsuri Shuar and the Achuar, amounting to approximately 38,000 people in 1983.

The Shuar successfully resisted the attempts of the Incas to subjugate them, and even after the Spanish conquest of America, the region remained largely unpacified and unsettled by Europeans. Though it was occasionally penetrated by military expeditions, religious missions and small-scale traders and gatherers of forest products, as late as 1870 there was only one permanent European settlement, Macas, in the Shuar area. They emerged from the 19th century with their cultural heritage relatively intact.

In the 20th century – and particularly since the 1950s – all this changed, as successive waves of missionaries, colonists and corporations washed across the Andes into the Ecuadorean *Oriente*. To consolidate their control, the missionaries of the Salesian order developed the strategy of abducting Shuar children and placing them in boarding schools under the direct supervision of the priests and isolated from their families. Another strategy was to concentrate the traditionally scattered Shuar population into villages located around the mission stations. By these means the missionaries expected to accelerate the 'civilising' process. The concentration of the Shuar into mission villages also made it easier for colonists to seize their lands. As a result of these practices, by the 1970s the Salesian order had become the most powerful political institution in the Shuar region, operating its own fleet of light aircraft, administering on behalf of the government a network of high schools, technical schools and hospitals, and exploiting for its own profit Shuar lands entrusted to it by the government. The success of the Salesians has attracted other missionaries, both Catholic (the Franciscans) and Protestant (the North American Gospel Missionary Union) to imitate their techniques.

On the heels of the missionaries have come colonists trying to escape from the problems of overpopulation and unjust land tenure in the *sierra*. The colonists have taken over large areas of former Shuar land with the support and assistance of the main government agency, the Ecuadorean Institute for Agrarian Reform and Colonisation (*Instituto Ecuatoriano de Reforma Agraria y Colonización*, IERAC, established in 1964 with the backing of the Alliance for Progress) and other agencies expressly set up to promote and facilitate the opening up of the *Oriente* to settlement, such as the Institute of Colonisation of the Ecuadorean Amazon Region (*Instituto de Colonización de la Región Amazónica Ecuatoriana*, INCRAE,

72

created in 1978). Finally, along with the colonists have come foreign corporations interested in exploiting the natural resources, especially oil, of the *Oriente*. Their activities, which are discussed in Appendix 4, have started to impinge on the Shuar region in the 1980s. The attitude of many of the colonists, missionaries and corporate managers to the Shuar is exemplified in the description of them given by one of the early Salesian missionaries, Father Calogera Guzmán. The typical Shuar was, he said, 'perfidious, cunning, selfish, vindictive, leisure- and pleasure-loving, enemy of every law and yoke that limits his complete freedom'.

It was in response to this kind of assault on their culture and homeland that the Shuar established in 1964 the Shuar Federation (*Federación de Centros Shuar*), combining the activities of various small associations and family centres which had developed in previous years around the town of Sucua. Initially, this was planned and carried out by the Salesians with the practical aim of counteracting the continuing advance of the colonists, which would have led to the extermination of the Shuar or their withdrawal deeper into the forest, and the collapse of the mission. However, some missionaries were also influenced by the newly-emerging liberation theology of the 1960s, which was forcing them to reappraise their role in relation to the Indians. This involved recognising past mistakes and consciously distancing themselves from the traditional alliance of the Church with the political and economic elites. It also meant moving away from the European roots of their theology in search of an 'indigenous Catholicism', which would acknowledge the validity of Shuar cultural traditions, and taking up the option of a genuine social change which would give the Indians control over their own lives.

The basic administrative unit of the Federation is the *centro*, a group of 25-30 families often related by marriage. On receiving official recognition, the *centro* can be granted its own land according to the number of members. Although not formally a village, as traditionally the Shuar live in scattered households, the *centro* nevertheless provides a focal point in the plaza or main square where there is a school and a teacher's house, a church, and a first-aid post. A sense of community is also provided by the regular meetings of all the members. The *centros* are grouped into associations (an average of eight in each), each of which has a president charged with implementing the Federation's policies. The Federation, which meets once a year in Sucua, coordinates the activities of the various associations.

The Federation's most important activity is concerned with defending and securing property titles for its members. Land titles are

73

granted in the name of the *centro* rather than to individuals. This reduces the risk of loss of the community's land to colonists through sale or despoilation, and also enables the *centro's* lands to be distributed in accordance with the needs of its members. However, obtaining clear title to its land can be a slow and expensive business, and the Shuars' hold on their lands is still far from secure.

Under the Federation a major change has taken place in the structure of the Shuar economy. There has been a shift away from dependence on subsistence farming and the collection of forest products towards a market-oriented economy based on cattle-ranching, which is at the moment the major source of income. The management of this industry is carried on by co-operatives based in the various *centros* and consisting of about a dozen members each. Cattle are bought with the aid of credits from the Federation, which also provides veterinary services, markets the produce in Sucua and Cuenca and on contract to the air force, and supervises the distribution of profits. The profits have enabled many *centros* to improve their facilities and strengthened their hold on their lands. But there have been many criticisms of the introduction of cattle as inappropriate to the Indians' traditional way of life and because of the lack of adequate marketing outlets. The project has been heavily promoted by the US Agency for International Development, has had adverse ecological consequences and its economic usefulness has been questioned.

The importance of the Federation in defending its members can be seen from the fate of those Shuar (just under a third in the late 1970s) who are not members. As colonisation has spread, an incipient class society with a system of labour and land tenure typical of the *sierra* has appeared in the *Oriente*. White and *mestizo* (mixed Indian and white) landowners form a dominant class and the dispossessed Shuar have been turned into landless labourers who are able to enter society only by abandoning their own culture, and are trapped at the lowest level with little chance of social mobility because social status is closely linked with racial origin.

An important activity of the Federation is in education. Mission and state education systems have been seen as the purveyors of alien and disorienting values not relevant to the realities of Shuar life, with teaching in Spanish and textbooks designed for use by the urban children of the coast or *sierra*. In response to this, the Federation operates a system of radio schools based on its own radio station, HCSK, which was established in Sucua in 1972. It transmits on several channels for 16 hours a day to the local schools programmes aimed at both children and adults (adult illiteracy among the Shuar was around

74

34 per cent in the late 1970s), and covers basic literacy and the elementary school syllabus. In the local schools, teaching is done alternately in Shuar and Spanish, using textbooks prepared by the Shuar staff of the radio station and adapted to the circumstances of Shuar children. The value of the radio teaching is unquestionable. The teaching schedule is adapted to the routine of the family; children are not separated from their families during their education and the location of a school in the *centro* makes education accessible to most children. The bilingual education programmes do not downgrade the Shuar's own language but at the same time give them the means to deal with the wider society around them. It is also cheap, about half the cost per pupil of that in the state system elsewhere in the country. The education programme is also supplemented with financial assistance for students to go on to high school and university, and the Federation publishes books and periodicals which aim to increase cultural awareness, and a bilingual newspaper, *Chicham*.

Another major area of activity is in health, where, because of lack of government interest and resources, the Federation has organised its own training courses for health volunteers, nurses and social workers. The emphasis of health care is on preventive medicine and the promotion of knowledge about hygiene. Information on health matters is broadcast by the radio station, which also supplies a first-aid kit to each *centro*. Besides the permanent health assistant based in each *centro*, the associations also have a team of health officials who can be mobilised to carry out vaccination campaigns in the event of outbreaks of contagious disease. The whole health programme is supervised by a medical team based at Sucua, and by the early 1980s its benefits were becoming clear in a general improvement of the health of the Shuar and a decrease in child mortality.

As a result of these initiatives, the Federation has succeeded in promoting a new awareness of Shuar culture and an awakening of Shuar identity which has been taking place in the last 15 years or so. After half a century of copying the values, behaviour and dress of the colonists, the Shuar are reasserting themselves and taking pride in their own cultural inheritance. At the same time, by making strategic adaptations to the realities of the wider society, they have given themselves an improved chance of long-term survival as a people.

We have seen how *barrio* women and rural Indians have mobilised to defend themselves and advance their claims to better treatment from the system. These are not the only cases; other popular responses to the system are visible at various levels and in various parts of the country. Together they add up to a growing chorus of demands from the 'forgotten majority' to have their urgent needs attended to by Ecuador's ruling elites, and to show that, given the chance and the resources, they have the determination and capacity to change their conditions of life for the better.

5. Andean Thatcherism

When Febres Cordero visited Washington in January 1986, he was fulsomely praised by the US President for applying free market solutions to Ecuador's recession-hit economy. Febres, declared Ronald Reagan, was 'an articulate champion of free enterprise' and his country 'a model debtor'. He promised that Ecuador would be amongst the first recipients of new loans under a plan designed by US Treasury Secretary James Baker to assist developing countries to liberalise their economies and remove restrictions on foreign trade and investment. At the same time, the World Bank's 'policy-based' loans confirmed Ecuador's new status as 'the international bankers' pet'. This image, so carefully cultivated by Febres during his first year in office, had a hollow ring in a country where living standards have been sharply cut in order to meet foreign debt repayments, and where the government rides roughshod over the opposition, pushes the constitution to its limits and violates human rights.

The Right's White Haired Hope

The key to the trauma which Ecuador's fragile democracy has experienced between 1984 and 1988 is to be found in the volatile personality of León Febres Cordero and the unwillingness of the far right to accept the norms of democratic behaviour. A US-trained engineer and self-made millionaire, Febres rose to prominence in the 1970s as head of the economic empire of Ecuador's richest man, Luis Noboa. As President of Guayaquil's Chamber of Industry, he spoke for the coastal oligarchy and was a tenacious and outspoken opponent of the Roldós-Hurtado governments. Possessed of a notoriously short temper to match his unruly white hair and rabble-rousing oratory, *El León* (the lion), as he likes to be known, took office armed with a

Thatcher-like political vision and determination, and a scant regard for the niceties of consensus and compromise.

Febres inherited an economy in recession, buffeted by a combination of falling oil prices and the consequences of the floods which affected agricultural production and exports in 1983. The philosophy which underpinned his 'reconstructionist' economic model reflected the President's own business background and the promises and commitments he had made to coastal business and banking interests during the election campaign. His first cabinet, made up of Guayaquil private sector representatives and ardent free marketeers, was a clear sign of the policies to be pursued to promote free enterprise and win the approval and support of Washington and the international banking community. The economic programme, described by Industry Minister Javier Niera as 'humanised, modern and progressive capitalism based on the social market economy', aimed to reduce state intervention, restrict public spending and increase incentives for the private sector. Priority was to be given to promoting exports, attracting foreign investment and renegotiating the foreign debt.

The 'opening up' of Ecuador's economy that followed, inevitably brought the country into conflict with her partners in regional and international organisations. Febres signed an agreement with the Overseas Private Investment Corporation (OPIC) in November 1984 which guaranteed US investors against nationalisation or expropriation. This agreement ran counter to the principles of the Andean Pact's Decision 24 and immediately strained relations between Ecuador and the other members. Subsequent 'revisionist' measures exempted foreign companies that exported 80 per cent or more of their production from the requirement to transform their Ecuadorean subsidiaries into mixed consortia or national companies. In 1985 Febres went on the attack, threatening to withdraw Ecuador from the Andean Pact if Decision 24 was not amended and the Pact's tariff structure reformed in a less protective direction.

Foreign oil companies were among the first to benefit from the open door strategy, when CEPE's 12 year monopoly of oil exploration was cancelled and multinational companies awarded up to 100 per cent tax relief on equipment as part of a drive to double known oil reserves by 1988. Foreign investment incentives featured prominently in a new Mining Law which was directed towards boosting the country's mineral potential, and a state mining corporation (INEMIN) was created to promote mixed operations under the most favourable tax and royalty regulations. The downward spiral of the oil price in the international market not only undermined hopes of sustained

78

Ecuador's Debt Crisis

In the 1970s Ecuador's military leaders borrowed heavily from foreign banks eager to lend to what they regarded as a good credit risk, due to its status as an oil exporter. But when, in the early 1980s, the collapse of oil prices and the contraction in demand for its traditional agricultural exports coincided with record interest rates in the US, Ecuador began to experience increasing difficulties in repaying its creditors. By 1981, Ecuador's debt, though small by Latin American standards, stood at twice the annual level of exports and swallowed up more than a quarter of the budget in servicing payments alone. Suddenly the economy faced one of the worst crises in the country's history and the government was forced to renegotiate the debt with foreign creditors and impose strict austerity at home. A 16 per cent decline in export revenues in 1982 brought a swift dose of IMF medicine in the shape of import curbs, currency devaluation, public spending cuts and higher prices. In an effort to stave off a rash of bankruptcies the Central Bank took responsibility for all private sector dollar debts, allowing debtors to pay the Central Bank in fast-depreciating *sucres*. This, the so-called 'sucretisation of the debt', was criticised by the Left as 'welfare for the rich', as it amounted to the Ecuadorean state bailing out private sector companies.

From 1983-86, Ecuador entered into a series of complicated rescheduling packages with its creditor banks designed to roll-over some of its debt obligations and extend the period of repayment. Although the terms of new loans were gradually relaxed, by 1986 Ecuador's total debt had risen to US$8.6 billion, and the amount of money it paid every year to service the debt reached an estimated 31 per cent of export revenues.

Ecuador's Total External Debt and Debt Service Ratio, 1977-87
(US$ billion)

	Debt	Debt Service Ratio*
1977	2.1	5
1978	3.2	11
1979	3.7	14
1980	4.8	18
1981	5.8	23
1982	6.2	30
1983	6.9	27
1984	7.2	31
1985	7.8	27
1986	8.6	31
1987	9.6**	31**

*Debt payments as a percentage of exports
**Preliminary estimates

Source: Economic Commission for Latin America and the Carribbean, *Notas sobre la Economía y el Desarrollo*, Santiago, Chile, various years.

economic growth but jeopardised Ecuador's relations with OPEC. Arguing that Ecuador's oil output was too small to have a significant impact on the world market, the government demanded an increase of 100,000 barrels per day in its production quota, and threatened to quit the cartel if the demand was not accepted. In fact, Ecuador's output was already 50 per cent over the OPEC quota as a result of Hurtado's efforts to maximise oil exports and counteract the effect of lower unit prices. It is apparent that Ecuador's vulnerability to fluctuations in the oil price is as acute as it ever was to fluctuations in cocoa, coffee or banana prices. In the mid-1980s oil accounted for more than 60 per cent of foreign earnings, and a one-dollar fall in the price per barrel abroad meant a 60 million dollar loss in annual export revenues. When the oil price came down from an average of 25.86 dollars a barrel in 1985 to around 11 dollars a barrel by the second quarter of 1986, Ecuador's oil revenues for the year fell by just under a billion dollars and caused what Vice-President Blasco Peñaherrera called 'the worst financial and economic crisis in Ecuador's history'. The possibility that prices will remain low and that the country will cease to be an oil exporter by the early 1990s are the twin spectres that spurred the Febres government like its predecessor, to give priority to the search for substantial new reserves.

Worst of all, the sharp deterioration in the country's financial position began to imperil the government's carefully nurtured relationship with the international bankers. The policies of adjustment in an 'open' direction and the undertaking to be 'responsible' about debt repayments had smoothed the renegotiation in 1986 of Ecuador's 7.8 billion dollar foreign debt with 400 foreign banks led by Chase Manhattan. By the standards of international loans, the terms were generous: 4.6 billion dollars of debt falling due in 1985-89 were rescheduled over 12 years and new loans of 200 million dollars were secured. After the refinancing package, ministers tried to take credit for reducing Ecuador's debt repayment burden. In fact, servicing the debt still amounted to almost a third of export earnings. Ecuador was receiving what Finance Minister Francisco Swett called 'the support and political solidarity of the US Treasury' and was the first country to benefit from the Baker Plan, receiving funds to meet its foreign obligations and make up for the shortfall in oil earnings. This preferential treatment reflected the value the Reagan administration placed on the region's only elected President committed to the free market model, and the importance for Washington of the Ecuadorean example of a 'responsible' approach to debt management. The price, of course, has been subservience to US foreign policy abroad, and social and institutional crisis at home.

Foreign Policy; the Shepherd and his Lamb

Within barely more than a year in office Febres had made three visits to Washington, prompting his critics to taunt that the Ecuadorean lamb (*cordero* is the Spanish word for lamb) was surrendering national interests to those of his northern shepherd. Indeed Ecuador soon acquired the reputation of being Reagan's staunchest and most reliable ally in Latin America. Febres won the plaudits of Washington for his opposition to proposals for a collective rescheduling of Latin America's foreign debt, the 'debtors' club' approach advocated not only by revolutionary governments such as Cuba's but also by such reformist regimes as that of Alan García of Peru. Washington approved, too, his defiance of OPEC and his tough stance on opening up the Andean Pact. Most of all, they welcomed his support for Reagan's Central American policy. In a typically abrasive and off-the-cuff remark, Febres declared that peace could only be restored in Central America after 'legitimate' elections had been held in Nicaragua. The Sandinista leader Daniel Ortega responded by calling Febres 'a tool of the United States' and questioning his own electoral methods and democratic credentials. Characteristically losing his temper, the Ecuadorean President impulsively severed diplomatic relations with Managua barely a week after Ecuador had joined the Contadora peace group's efforts to find a solution to the Central American crisis.

With foreign policy apparently made at the whim of the President, and Febres adopting increasingly right-wing and maverick positions, Ecuador blocked an Organisation of American States resolution condemning the Pinochet dictatorship in Chile, encouraged South Africa to open a trade mission in Quito and came near to suspending relations with New Delhi after allowing Sikh separatists to establish a bureau in the capital. Then, in an abrupt change of direction designed to disarm and outmanoeuvre his opponents and polish up Ecuador's tarnished image abroad, Febres paid a visit to Cuba to discuss trade-related issues claiming that his domestic critics were failing to appreciate and grasp national interests. Aside from his uncritical support for the US, it was increasingly difficult to see a consistent foreign policy on the part of the Febres government, and its spontaneous and improvised character weakened Ecuador's position in those regional and international groupings where its natural friends and allies should be found.

Restructuring the Economy

As part of the programme to reduce state intervention and stimulate exports, the government slashed the levels of protection being given to local industry. The tariff regime was overhauled and protection for local manufacturers limited to a maximum of 80 per cent. The list of banned imports was slimmed down from 900 to fewer than 500 items and duties on imports with local equivalents lowered. The stated aim was to make locally produced manufactured goods more efficient and competitive. In fact, the measures raised the spectre of a sharply reduced manufacturing sector decimated by a combination of foreign competition and high interest rates. Changes were made in the Industrial Development Law to permit the privatisation of firms in the state sector and make free trade zones more attractive to foreign investors. Hurtado had set up the free trade zones, but only one in Esmeraldas had so far been designated and this had failed to attract the anticipated inflow of capital, probably because of the proximity of similar zones in Panama and Brazil. Local industry was already suffering from falling domestic demand, increased competition from abroad and shortages of foreign exchange. It slid still further into recession when at the end of January 1986, the government announced a substantial increase in value added tax, more reductions in import duties and a 14 per cent devaluation of the *sucre*.

While industrialists were feeling the cold wind of monetarist 'realism' and 'readjustment', agricultural exporters were basking in the sunshine of monetarist 'comparative advantage'. Government might expose domestic industry to the rigours of foreign competition, but it cossetted export-oriented agriculture. Guaranteed minimum prices for growers, the provision of credit and technical assistance to renew old plantations (Ecuador had lost its position as the world's largest banana producer in 1983) and a floating exchange rate for the calculation of export earnings, all helped to boost agricultural exports. With bananas, cocoa, coffee and shrimp exporters receiving such favourable treatment, non-oil exports rose in 1985 by a quarter to 978 million dollars. Ecuador regained its position as the world's leading banana producer, assisted in part by disease, climatic and labour problems among rival growers.

Producers benefited again in 1986 when the devaluation brought on by the economic crisis was accompanied by a 15 per cent hike in agricultural prices. As usual, the big landowners and the well-connected did best out of these measures. Small farmers and those not in the export sector suffered by contrast from a dearth of credit and high interest rates. The Federation of Agricultural Workers of the

Littoral declared at its VI Congress in 1985 that 'the peasants must be freed from the debt noose of official creditors ... who are very exacting and severe in regard to small proprietors, yet very flexible and lenient towards big ones'.

In mid-1986 Finance Minister Alberto Dahik acknowledged that, although there had been a slight strengthening of oil prices, the era of large oil surpluses had probably ended. This meant a new austerity package, which was originally announced in August, after the mid-term elections had been got out of the way in June. When it was published, the details of the letter of intent made bleak reading for workers, peasants and industrialists alike. Public expenditure (which had actually risen under Febres in spite of his monetarist rhetoric) was to be cut by five per cent, while debt service repayments were to be maintained. Another round of import liberalisation measures was decreed, coupled with relaxation of controls on interest rates and a further devaluation of the currency.

Febres' economic strategy had been based on cementing an alliance between the domestic business elite and international capital. Even if it had worked as the monetarists in his government claimed it should, it paid little or no attention to the real conditions of life and needs of the mass of the population and left them with only vague and fragile promises of future well-being. The economic crisis of 1986 wrecked even this strategy, and the rising tide of popular opposition and protest became more and more difficult to contain. During the opening years of his government, Febres had been able to diffuse protest against the social and economic costs of his free market policies by employing strong-arm tactics and exploiting divisions among his opponents. During the first six months of the Febres administration, the FUT organised three anti-government general strikes. The first, which Febres denounced as 'illegal and subversive', was called in October 1984 to protest the first round of IMF austerity measures, but its effect was blunted by the non-participation of the oil and transport workers. The second, a two-day strike in January 1985 against rising living costs brought on by government authorised price increases, was again denounced as illegal by Febres. When arms and explosives were discovered near Quito during the strike, he tried to discredit the unions by accusing them of complicity with terrorist groups.

The third general strike in March 1985 had a more overtly political tone and called for the defence of democracy as well as higher wages. The government's hostile reaction to this growing militancy and its willingness to use troops and police to evict forcibly workers occupying factories certainly blunted the effectiveness of the protests, as did the absence of key groups of workers. Frequent mobilisations also ran the risk that the rank and file members would grow weary of regular strike calls which seemed to achieve little but exposed them to the danger of violent retaliation. However, as the economic crisis escalated during 1986, so did the tempo of FUT protests. The fifth general strike against Febres effectively brought the country to a standstill, and with key transport workers supporting the action for the first time, the unions were able to claim a 90 per cent response to the call for a stoppage. The authorities countered by arresting five of the top union leadership and many hundreds of demonstrators, while Febres lashed out at the Congress which, he claimed, had become 'the submissive and obedient tool of the extreme left-wing groups who hate democracy'.

Who Rules in Quito?

The period from Febres' inauguration in August 1984 to the June 1986 mid-term elections were a testing time for Ecuador's democratic institutions. This was because of the permanent conflict between the President and the legislature, where the opposition parties ID, DP, FADI, MPD, PRE and a PD faction (which between them held a majority of the seats) formed a *Bloque Democrático Progresista*

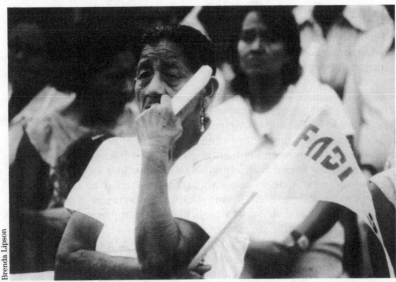

Brenda Lipson

A puzzling time for the voters.

84

(BDP). It was also because of Febres' own preference for adversarial rather than consensus politics. His abrasive and authoritarian style provoked one ex-minister to comment that Ecuadoreans were living in a 'Rambo-cracy', while former President Hurtado described the Febres government as 'a dictatorship with a constitutional fig-leaf'.

On the surface, the first year and a half of the administration was occupied by a series of constitutional crises in which the two branches of government clashed over who had the right to interpret the constitution. In fact the conflicts were political in origin and revealed fundamental disagreements over economic and social policy.

The first issue to cause a rift between the two sides was the appointment of Supreme Court judges. The crisis came to a head when the Congress voted to reduce the judges' term of office from six to four years, ruled that the current incumbents had completed their stint and proceeded to elect 16 new members of the court. Febres and his allies in the FRN contested the legality of these appointments and backed the original members in spite of a ruling by the court's own president that the legislature had acted constitutionally. When the new judges attempted to take their seats, Febres ordered police to prevent their entry into the Palace of Justice. The dispute was eventually resolved only after four months of heated exchanges when Febres and the opposition leader Raúl Baca agreed to the resignation of both sets of judges and the appointment of 16 replacements. While the outcome could be interpreted as a climbdown by the opposition, and to some extent by the President as well, incalculable damage had been inflicted on the prestige of the political system. The Congress' image was badly tarnished by the disruptive behaviour of the FRN deputies, who resorted to tactics ranging from cutting microphone cables and brandishing guns in the chamber to staging frequent walk-outs and boycotts of debates. They also packed the chamber with large numbers of their supporters who barracked the opposition and made the work of Congress impossible, and were also used to attack and intimidate journalists and opposition deputies. The opposition claimed that this was all part of an orchestrated attempt to discredit the legislature in the eyes of the public as a prelude to its closure and the establishment of a dictatorship. There is no doubt that the prestige and credibility of the democratic process was damaged by the existence of two Supreme Courts, the highly public and acrimonious dialogue between government and opposition, and the accusations of anti- or unconstitutional behaviour each side hurled at each other.

The political deal which ended the crisis was strictly a short-term one. The powers of the respective branches of government remained unclear and undefined and the likelihood of future collisions

85

remained. While the BDP justified its retreat on the grounds that it had acted to preserve democracy, it could not hide its growing concern about defections from the ranks of the opposition. These *cambios de camiseta* (literally 'changing shirts') were skilfully exploited by Febres, who used the President's power of patronage to build up a block of pro-government 'independents' without party affiliation. On his frequent trips to the provinces he concluded deals, offered handouts and dispensed larger slices of the state budget in return for political support. By these means, during his first year in power he induced 11 deputies to abandon their party militancy, and by the middle of 1985 he had created a slim and unstable working majority in the Congress. This was a considerable achievement and a tribute to Febres' political skills. However, the ease with which elected representatives abandoned their party loyalties and the platforms on which they had been elected confirms the fundamental failure to create a modern and disciplined party system and highlights the deep-rooted assumption that Congressmen represent only themselves.

The next major confrontation followed the 1985 New Year round of price rises. Febres ignored the demand for a 15,000 *sucre* monthly minimum wage which formed the main plank of the FUT's call for a general strike, and announced a new level of 8,500 *sucres* in March. The Congress reacted by holding an extraordinary session which fixed the new minimum at 10,000 *sucres*. Febres then lodged a claim with the *Tribunal de Garantiás Constitucionales* (Tribunal of Constitutional Guarantees, TGC) that the Congress had acted illegally in calling the emergency session. When the TGC ruled in favour of the legislature, the President accused it of acting in a partisan manner, vetoed the congressional decision and published his own proposal in the official gazette. Once again, behind the legalistic arguments and accusations of violation of the constitution lay a fundamental disagreement over economic policy. Febres justified the small increase as a necessary element in the government's economic strategy and required under the IMF terms for the renegotation of the external debt. The congressional proposal he dismissed as dangerously inflationary. The opposition countered that in the absence of price controls the minimum wage he established was insufficient to meet even the basic needs of wage-earners and their families, and that it was unjust that the poor should be made to pay the cost of servicing the foreign debt.

At the end of his first year in office, Febres could review his situation with some satisfaction. The main planks of his 'reconstructionist' economic policies were in place. He had inflicted two major political defeats on the opposition, and deals with individual deputies and with the CFP and the FRA had conjured up a small pro-government majority in the Congress (37 votes out of 71). The election of the CFP leader Averroes Bucaram as President of the Congress ensured that any censure motions could be stage-managed so as not to embarass the government. Febres could now turn his attention to the mid-term elections scheduled for January 1986; the loss of only a handful of seats would rob him of his hard-won majority. His preference was to postpone the elections and preserve his advantage for the rest of his term, but there was no way he could muster the necessary two-thirds majority for this in the Congress. Instead, a package of amendments to the electoral law was pushed through, which postponed the poll for six months on the grounds that the time was needed for the electoral rolls to be renewed.

The change in the electoral timetable gave Febres two important advantages. It allowed him, firstly, to call a plebiscite to coincide with the June poll and, secondly, to launch a campaign to discredit his opponents by linking them to an upsurge in guerrilla violence. The President hoped to build up a 'third force' consisting of independents and thereby create a more dependable base of political support. Given the low level of party membership among the electorate and the weakness of party loyalty, it looked as if a skilfully worded question asking whether independents could be elected to public office without the requirement of party affiliation 'thus confirming the equality of all Ecuadoreans before the law' would have a good chance of winning a 'yes' vote in the plebiscite. Meanwhile a wave of terrorist actions by the *Alfaro Vive, Carajo*(AVC) guerrilla movement, culminating in the kidnapping of a leading Guayaquil banker, Nahim Isaías, gave the government the excuse it wanted for a crackdown on 'subversion' and the formation of a new anti-terrorist police unit. Under Febres' personal direction the security forces stormed the AVC hideout, killing four guerrillas and their hostage. Febres attempted to capitalise on the kidnapping and violence by suggesting that the guerrillas were 'sheltered in high places' and pointedly denounced Osvaldo Hurtado as 'an agent of international subversion'.

If the President hoped to gain from these slurs on his opponents, his tactics backfired. Not only did he lose his majority in the elections, but the constitutional reform was resoundingly rejected in the plebiscite. Of the 59 seats contested, Febres' PSC took 15 and retained its position as the second largest party, but the ID and its allies took 35 seats. The President's support in the Congress slumped to 19 while the opposition could now rally 43 deputies. The two parties that had given him his narrow majority up till now, the CFP and the FRA, failed in their attempt to distance themselves from the government during the

Violations of human rights in Ecuador

Although the powerful and well-connected in Ecuador have always oppressed the poor and weak, the country has on the whole not suffered from the sort of gross, systematic and widespread violations of human rights associated with the military governments of Brazil, Argentina, Colombia and Uruguay at various times in the last 20 years. State-sponsored or state sanctioned terrorism has been relatively unknown. However, in the last few years there has been a worrying trend towards arbitrary and illegal actions by the security forces with the government turning a blind eye. In May 1986 Amnesty International reported on the human rights situation as follows:

'Suspects have been seized without warrants and their detentions denied to have occurred while they were interrogated, usually for between 24 and 72 hours. Prisoners were frequently reported to have been seized by plainclothes police of the *Servicio de Investigación Criminal* (SIC), briefly interrogated, and then transferred to secret military interrogation centres. Some who had been seized in Quito reported after their release that they had been blindfolded and driven for about 40 minutes to a centre they believed to be in Conocoto, Valle de los Chillos, for prolonged interrogation under torture.

'... teacher Marco Banalcázar Gómez was detained without warrant on 24 October 1985 in Ibarra and his whereabouts were unknown for four days... He had been taken to an isolated house in Yahuarcocha for interrogation. During the first day there he was hoisted by ropes tied first to his thumbs then to his middle fingers, kicked and punched, and had his head held in a tank of cold water. The following day he was again suspended by his thumbs, nearly asphyxiated by having a lemon forced into his mouth while Coca Cola was poured into his nostrils, and cut with a knife. On the evening of 26 October he was taken to SIC headquarters and beaten again. On 28 October he was required to sign a statement and then returned to Ibarra ...On 4 November an Ibarra court dismissed the charge of involvement in an AVC extortion case and he was released.

'... the Government of Ecuador has initiated no investigations in the past year in response to evidence of torture or unacknowledged detention in political cases but has stressed the "guilt" of the alleged victim. In September 1985 President León Febres Cordero said that "those who live within the Constitution and the law" enjoyed absolute respect for their human rights.'

In August 1987, participants in the V National Forum on Human Rights, held in Guayaquil, denounced the police authorities for having initiated 'a dirty war similar to that in other countries of the South American Cone'. ▶

> According to Sister Elsie Monge, President of the Ecumenical Commission of Human Rights, between July 1986 and August 1987 there were reported 39 cases of homicide committed by 'elements of the public forces', 204 arbitrary arrests, 88 cases of torture, 65 cases of secret detention, 25 unauthorised residential violations, and 50 land disputes, some of which included the assassination of leaders and the destruction of homes and fields by armed groups.
>
> Sources: *Amnesty International Newsletter*, May 1986; *Andean Commission of Jurists Newsletter*, September 1987

campaign and polled less than seven and four per cent of the vote respectively. The once all-conquering CFP seemed to have disintegrated completely.

The government's defeat was directly related to the deepening economic and political crisis during the first half of the year. The fall in oil revenues necessitated savage deflationary measures at a sensitive political moment. Cutbacks in social expenditure and substantial increases in the prices of such basic foodstuffs as milk, butter, rice and sugar caused widespread popular resentment and added weight to the opposition criticism that the abandonment of price controls had fuelled inflation. The government had successfully attracted World Bank and other loans but earmarked them to cover balance of payments deficits and repay foreign debts instead of maintaining living standards. The voters were issuing a clear message to the President that however well his economic policies might go down abroad, they were deeply unpopular at home.

A further cause of disenchantment arose from the opposition's charges that Febres was behaving like a dictator and tampering with the constitution to gain partisan political advantage. The President's credibility also suffered from his attempts to link opposition groups, especially student and labour militants, with guerrilla subversion and drug dealing. In common with its neighbours in the region, Ecuador experienced an alarming rise in crime, violence and drug trafficking during the 1980s. Febres' government cracked down hard on the AVC group (which has links with the Colombian M-19 movement) and another splinter group, *Montoneros Patria Libre* (MPL). The highly-publicised suppression of these undoubtedly active guerrilla groups was coupled with a wider attack on other 'subversives' whose only offences were to oppose the government, and there was a growing chorus of complaint about the security forces' violations of human rights. A highly critical report by Amnesty International has detailed 'a

'The most macho general in South America'
Frank Vargas Pazzos

General Frank Vargas Pazzos is a figure firmly within a well-established Ecuadorean political tradition of turbulent populist leaders with an authoritarian but indeterminate ideology and a macho personal style. He is a presidential candidate in the 1988 elections, though not one of the frontrunners.

Vargas Pazzos' immediate background reads like something out of Gabriel García Márquez' *Cien Años de Soledad*. His late father, Colonel Luis Vargas Yepez, was a notable liberal in his time and fought, arms in hand, for the cause on various occasions. He also found time between his political activities and managing the family *hacienda* 'Medio Mundo' (half the world) to sire 71 other children besides the 12 he had by his wife Doña Ida Pazzos. The Vargas clan practically forms a political movement on its own.

Frank Vargas reached the top rank in the air force not so much because of his service record – which contains several incidents of insubordination and lack of discipline – as in spite of it. An officer of unimpeachable moral character and regarded as outstanding in his profession for his intelligence, talent and ability, it has been said that 'he is the kind of officer whom you don't know whether to shoot or to decorate'. He is popular with the soldiers under his command, as his clashes with the government in 1987 demonstrated. Married twice, he has 10 children whose potpourri of exotic and un-Spanish names (Gina, Daisy, Frank, Silvia, another Frank, Vladimir, Miluska, Yael, Daniel Espartico and Yuri) is itself a clue to the vagueness and lack of clarity of his views. He is a karate expert and an enthusiast for duelling with the machete. At various times, he has undergone advanced training as a pilot and as a staff officer in the US, Venezuela, Panama and Spain. He has also been a military attaché in London.

His insubordinate temperament first manifested itself when he was a cadet at the Military College in the 1950s; he was expelled for physically assaulting a senior officer whom he thought was mistreating the cadets. On another occasion, when he was a lieutenant at the air force base in Taura, he wanted to air his complaints about the living conditions of his men to Velasco Ibarra during a presidential visit. Velasco waved the young lieutenant aside and turned away from him, at which point Vargas ordered his men to train their weapons on the President, and forced him at gunpoint to listen to his complaints. When a well-known conservative, Simón Ribadaneira, notorious for carrying a pistol and firing it in the Congress, asked him to arrange flights to his constituency during an election, Vargas offered to arm-wrestle him and then challenged him to a duel with knives as a condition of granting his request.

His latest clash with the political establishment came as a result of his denunciation in 1986 of corruption and bribe-taking by senior military men ▶

> and politicians during the purchase of new aircraft for the military airline. When the government failed to pursue his allegations, Vargas withdrew to the Manta air force base in Manabí. When the guarantees given him were ignored, he escaped and seized the Mariscal Sucre air force base in Quito. The army was called out and assaulted the base. Five people were killed in the fighting, a number of others wounded, and more than 400 arrested. In January 1987, during a presidential visit to the Taura air force base, Febres Cordero was seized by paratroopers loyal to Vargas and held hostage for 12 hours against the release of the General.
>
> Though he predicted that Febres would not complete his presidential mandate, Vargas denies that he is a *golpista* (ie would carry out a coup) and insists that he has acted in defence of his men, for the honour of the armed forces, and in the interests of the people. The majority of the armed forces 'are morally on the side of my ideas and my thesis ... I choose to fight and I know I will win, we are going to overthrow the tyranny ... We've reached an incredible situation in Ecuador, a concentration of wealth so brutal that 15 or 16 families control the economy of the country, what matters is not that they control it but the way they administer the wealth ... Conflict should be resolved within the law, but if it can't be and the response to lawful complaints is repression, persecution, state assassination, I believe any free citizen has the answer: the principle of self-defence ... As for the question, would I take up arms, it depends on the tyrant. Either he should change his ways or he should resign to prevent a confrontation ... citizen Febres Cordero once invited me to stage a coup against President Osvaldo Hurtado, and I refused.'

wave of torture cases involving police and military agencies in major Ecuadorean cities'. Amnesty's findings have been corroborated by the Quito-based Catholic Ecumenical Human Rights Commission (CEDHU), which confirmed that arbitrary arrest, prison brutality and illegal nighttime raids carried out by masked agents are on the increase. CEDHU's records show that in 1986 there were 58 cases of torture, 165 cases of arbitrary arrest, 33 of unauthorised police raids. There have been over 100 deaths caused by police and security agents, and various unexplained 'disappearances' since Febres took office. Those arrested and detained have reported the use of the *polea* to suspend and spreadeagle the prisoner, of asphyxiation, and electric shocks to the genitals and other parts of the body during interrogation.

The Hour of the General

The spectre of a fresh bout of military interventionism was briefly raised when the armed forces commander Frank Vargas Pazzos, a flamboyant and popular general with presidential ambitions, staged a short-lived revolt. Although not a direct threat to democracy, the rebellion proved an acute embarassment to the government and Febres came under fire for his handling of the affair. Vargas claimed that his insubordination was designed to expose corruption and anti-democratic plotting by the Defence Minister, General Luis Piñeiros, and the army chief, General Manuel Albuja. The impact of the rebellion was dissipated when Vargas withdrew to the Mariscal Sucre air base near Quito, barricaded himself in there, and appealed to the people to protect the occupants. The government mobilised the army and assaulted the base, with five dead, many wounded and more than 400 arrested in the incident. However, investigations into his allegations of corruption, in particular concerning bribes associated with the purchase of a Fokker aircraft for the military-run airline TAME, put several of Febres' appointees under a cloud. The government's obvious reluctance to pursue an enquiry into the affair and its counter-charges of embezzlement against Vargas, provoked public and congressional criticism. While the democratic system seemed so far to have survived the revolt without a major crisis, the fallout from the Vargas affair continued to sour relations between Febres and the opposition. When the *Bloque Progresista* voted in favour of an amnesty for Vargas, the President and senior officers opposed the move on the grounds that his crimes were military, not political, in nature.

The Congress, strong and confident in its substantial anti-government majority, now began to attack the embattled President on all fronts. Febres' foreign policy was censured for having 'a clear attachment to the government of Ronald Reagan' and for isolating Ecuador from international and regional organisations. Inspired by the example of Alan García's government in Peru and following a speech by the socialist deputy Diego Delgado (who claimed that 'every 33 minutes an Ecuadorean child dies and at the same time the country pays 6.2 *sucres* in servicing its foreign debt'), the Congress proposed that a ceiling of 25 per cent of oil earnings be placed on debt repayments. The church added its voice to the public concern about the future of democracy when a conference of bishops criticised the 'wave of immoral administrative actions' which was sweeping the country.

The fiercest clash occurred over the IMF-inspired austerity package introduced in August 1986. Congress impeached Finance Minister Alberto Dahik, and after a month of remorseless questioning which caused his health to break down, forced him out of office. However, Febres swiftly negated Dahik's dismissal by appointing him to the post of principal economic adviser. With feelings running high Febres ignored the Congress' rejection of his 12,000 *sucre* minimum wage bill and published the law in the official gazette, just as he had done the previous year. Faced with a hostile and uncooperative legislature, the President increasingly resorted to actions of doubtful legality and outright intimidation. During the Dahik impeachment proceedings, police entered the chamber and disrupted a session by firing smoke bombs. On several occasions deputies were physically threatened and assaulted by pro-government mobs. In one instance Febres sent 15 urgent economic bills, some containing more than 200 clauses, to be dealt with by the Congress within the regulation two weeks, and they all became law in spite of the fact that the deputies had scarcely had any opportunity to debate the contents.

Reaping the Whirlwind

Febres took a strong stand during the Isaías kidnapping and the shootout with the AVC that followed, insisting that he would never negotiate with terrorists. On a visit to Washington, he was praised by President Reagan for his 'brave struggle' against international terrorism and the drug trade. But soon after his return from the US, Febres was seized at gunpoint by rebel paratroopers who supported Vargas Pazzos and held hostage for 12 hours at the Taura air base near Guayaquil until he promised to release Vargas from detention. Within days the Congress began impeachment proceedings against the President for negotiating with the rebels and dishonouring the nation. Neither side emerged with much credit from an incident which was now threatening to become the most serious threat to democracy since the departure of the generals in 1979. The Congress called on the President to resign for his behaviour during the crisis, in particular the lack of moral authority he displayed. Febres justified his actions with the claim that he had not bargained for his own life but for the sake of fellow hostages and for Ecuador. Once free, he said that as 'a man of honour' he would not prosecute his abductors, who were now under arrest at Fort Atahualpa, but would not stop the military from doing so. Critics claimed he was going back on his work, while Febres retorted that the congressional vote against him was 'irrelevant, anti-democratic and lacked any moral force'.

The Taura kidnapping once more focused attention on the role of the military in a crisis-torn democracy. In order to reimpose their authority, the military high command ignored the agreement the President signed with the rebels. The paratroopers were imprisoned, charged with treason, cowardice and endangering state security. In

93

the opinion of his opponents, Febres himself was responsible for generating the climate of aggression and violence to which he eventually fell victim. In the words of Rodrigo Borja, he 'reaped the fruits of his violence and his disrespect for the symbols and institutions of the democratic system'.

No sooner had Febres begun the work of repairing his shattered political image than a new disaster struck the Ecuadorean economy. On 5 and 6 March 1987 a succession of ten earthquakes or major tremors, followed by a series of landslides, mudslides and floods, devastated the eastern province of Napo and affected three others. More than 300 people were killed and 4,000 reported missing, and around 90,000 more lost their homes and property. The tremors wrecked roads and bridges, and a key pumping station and 30 miles of the Transamazonian oil pipeline from the major oilfield at Lago Agrio were destroyed. The government, which had already suspended debt repayments some weeks before the earthquake because of the fall in the petrol price, now faced a long period with no revenues at all from oil exports. With damage repair and loss of exports estimated at around 926 million dollars, the effect of the disaster was to push the economy further into recession, worsen the balance of payments deficit and increase inflationary pressures. Opposition leaders backed the President's call for national unity but the truce lasted less than a fortnight. A new package of measures which increased petrol prices by 80 per cent and urban and interprovincial transport by up to 40 per cent pushed food costs up sharply and provoked a general strike on 25 March to protest the measures. With an overtly political platform calling for a political trial of the President, the strike met with a strong response in the *sierra* but less enthusiasm in Guayas, Los Ríos and Manabí.

Conclusion

During his final year in office Febres became a 'lame duck' President, his popularity and political standing eroded by the cumulative political and economic crises of the opening months of 1987. The President's isolation increased when he was deserted by some of his most talented ministers and advisers, anxious to distance themselves from his record, and deprived of others by corruption charges and a growing chorus of criticism and questioning of the government's integrity.

In June 1987 former Industry Minister Xavier Niera went into hiding to avoid facing fraud charges; Finance Minister Domingo Córdovez,

94

among others, was accused of bribe-taking; and officials close to Febres, including his private secretary, were accused by opposition deputies of illegal enrichment arising from government contracts. Vice-President Blasco Peñaherrera joined those within the administration who felt a growing unease at the direction of government policy and Febres' style of crisis management, particularly his handling of the kidnap crisis and the seemingly endless wrangles with Congress.

The earthquake, which momentarily united the country, soon developed into a partisan issue. The controversy centred upon the role and ultimate intentions of some thousands of US troops who arrived in Ecuador at the request of the President to assist with post-earthquake reconstruction work. Congress regarded the presence of so many US troops as an affront to national sovereignty and viewed their motives with deep suspicion. Vargas Pazzos launched his bid for the presidency by warning that Ecuador was in danger of becoming another Honduras, and opposition deputies claimed knowledge of US plans for a military base on the Galápagos Islands and for a School of the Americas in the Amazon basin. The government's handling of the earthquake emergency prompted criticism that relief and welfare of the local population in the afflicted areas was taking second place to work on reconstruction of the oil pipeline. Aid (including £400,000 from Britain) found its way to the more accessible areas but did not always reach those most in need. There is evidence, for example, that tents intended as temporary accommodation for earthquake victims were in fact being used for the troops sent to rebuild the roads and bridges.

By far the greatest blow to Febres' policies came from the crippled economy. 1987 was the most disastrous year in the short history of the Ecuadorean oil industry. With oil output and revenues down by 60 per cent through a combination of pipeline damage and the decline in the world oil price, Ecuador was in no position to keep up the interest payments on its foreign debt. Negotiations with its creditors had already broken down before the earthquake, and forced Ecuador to suspend debt service repayments. Soon afterwards, and following the Peruvian example, it announced that it would limit the level of repayments to a proportion of its export revenues. The irony that a country once regarded by the international banking community as a 'model debtor' should find itself standing shoulder to shoulder with Alan García's Peru indicates that Ecuador could best tackle such a problem in tandem with neighbouring governments of the region, and that Febres' go-it-alone strategy did not work. Nevertheless, one of the first actions taken by the President once the oil pipeline came back into service in August was to make an interest payment on the outstanding debt and urgently conclude debt renegotiations with the creditor banks who obviously preferred to deal with Febres rather than a more nationalistic and less cooperative successor.

Frustrated at their continued inability to remove the President, the opposition took to impeaching his ministers instead. In October 1987 they called to account Interior Minister Luis Robles for the deteriorating human rights situation and for complicity in cases of torture, disappearance and arbitrary arrest. In reacting to the congressional challenge Febres showed he had lost none of his verbal combativeness despite recent reversals. He denounced the opposition ruling as 'unconstitutional' and 'illegal' on the grounds that all the necessary legal steps had not been completed in time and steadfastly refused to remove his Minister. Once again the two sides were locked in bitter, if ultimately impotent, conflict. The opposition, convinced that government agents had assaulted and badly beaten Robles' interrogator, Diego Delgado, accused the President of being present at interrogations when torture had been used.

As so often in the past, the discontent eventually spilled onto the streets. When the FUT organised a strike for 28 October they demanded not only higher wages but also Robles' removal and the sacking of Labour Minister Guillermo Chang. Their protests, which as usual met with a bigger response in the *sierra* than on the coast, were aimed at a government that had shown itself anxious to negotiate with foreign bankers but spent little time combatting unemployment and inflation. Indeed, the disastrous consequences arising from the government's policies were becoming ever more apparent in the official figures: inflation rising towards 35 per cent for 1987, the foreign debt standing at around US$9.5 billion, and unemployment at 13 per cent and rising. Only the resumption of full oil exports and OPEC's decision allowing Ecuador to exceed its production quota in order to compensate for losses over the previous six months, promised to lift the gloomy economic scenario.

Andean Thatcherism generated a new set of problems to add to Ecuador's perennial political and socio-economic ills. By opening up Ecuador to an unprecedented degree to the outside world Febres exposed it to the fluctuations in world trade. The fall in commodity prices, the contraction of world trade and the drying up of new loans and investment, cruelly bared Ecuador's new vulnerability. Certainly Ecuador, like other Latin American debtors, will find it difficult to maintain political stability if it cannot achieve economic growth and a fairer social distribution of wealth. There is little evidence, either, that nine years of democracy since 1979 have succeeded in transforming

96

Rodrigo Borja on the campaign trail.

Ecuador's political culture. Ten candidates contested the first round of the presidential elections and it was not encouraging that personality rather than policies predominated and there was little debate over how they intended to tackle the country's deep-seated problems. Nor should we forget that the country has experienced stable constitutional rule before, for more than eight years, and still could not prevent a reversion to coups d'etat and dictatorship.

Whatever the outcome of the elections, the new President will face seemingly intractable problems as Ecuador struggles to keep its fragile and unstable democracy together in a post-oil future; where powerful economic and military interests are uncommitted to its institutions and tempted to go for the simple solutions of dictatorship; where the mass of the population wait with increasing resentment and impatience for their urgent social and economic needs to be attended to; where the US government sees Ecuador as merely a pawn in its own global strategy; and where the international banks insist on their right to determine the country's economic priorities.

97

Appendix 1

Ecuador's Territorial and Maritime Disputes

Ecuador has been involved in disputes about national territory and frontiers which have led to several conflicts with other countries, and has usually been the loser in these, suffering massive amputations as a result. After independence in the early 1830s, the territory over which Ecuador claimed sovereignty covered approximately 714,860 sq.km. By the 1980s the territory under effective control amounted to 275,341sq.km. Unsatisfied claims, especially to the *Oriente* province lost in 1942 (all Ecuadorean public documents carry the slogan 'Ecuador always has been, is, and will be an Amazon country') are an important element in politics.

Conflicts with Peru

Following the independence of South America, Peru claimed that southern Ecuador was part of Peru and did not accept its forcible annexation to Colombia in 1822. Peru and Colombia were at war over this claim in 1828-29. During most of this war, until the defeat of Peru, Guayaquil was under Peruvian blockade or occupation. In 1842 Ecuador made a counter-claim to the Peruvian provinces of Jaen and Maynas. War was only averted by the fall of the Flores government in Ecuador, and the claim lapsed.

The major Ecuadorean-Peruvian territorial dispute – which is still unresolved – is over the *Oriente* (Amazon) region, and concerns about 174,500 sq.km. of territory stretching almost the entire length of the two countries' common frontier. This dispute began in 1854 when Ecuador, in an attempt to raise money to pay its foreign creditors and service the foreign debt, started to sell 'unused' lands in the Amazon to European colonists. Peru claimed sovereignty over the territory in question and demanded that Ecuador rescind the sales. In 1859 Peru invaded Ecuador while the country was involved in a civil war, occupied Guayaquil and forced one of the several rival governments to sign the Treaty of Mapasingue (1860), cancelling the Amazon contracts and and acknowledging Peruvian sovereignty there. When the civil war ended the Ecuadoreans under García Moreno succeeded in expelling the Peruvians. Ecuador never acknowledged the validity of the

Treaty of Mapasingue.

In 1887 Ecuador and Peru agreed to settle their frontier claims by arbitration, and this led to the García-Herrera Treaty of 1890, which gave Ecuador access to the river Marañon and hence to the Amazon. However towards the end of the 19th century, the expansion of world demand for rubber was giving the disputed Amazon region a new and greater economic significance, and the area allocated to Ecuador under the treaty turned out to be especially rich in rubber. The Peruvians consequently refused to confirm the treaty. A compromise boundary arbitrated by Spain in 1909 was not accepted, and in 1910 only strong pressure from Argentina, Brazil and the US prevented war breaking out between Ecuador and Peru, (incidentally, the modern weapons that Ecuador bought during that war scare were used instead in a bloody civil war in 1911-12, when more than 3,000 Ecuadoreans were killed). Attempts to have the dispute arbitrated by the US between 1924 and 1938 failed in the face of Peru's de facto occupation (through settlers and military detachments). Fighting broke out in July 1941 and by September the Peruvians controlled not just the area they claimed but also acknowledged Ecuadorean territory in the Amazon, and parts of the provinces of El Oro and Loja. The defeated Ecuadorean government, under pressure from the US (which wanted a quick settlement so as not to distract her in the midst of the crisis following the Japanese attack on Pearl Harbour) signed the Río Protocol, by which she lost more than half her claimed national territory to Peru, including the access to the Marañon.

Ecuadorean opinion never accepted the 'Protocol of Sacrifice', and immediately on becoming President in 1960, Velasco Ibarra officially denounced it. In the early 1970s the disputed territory took on still greater signficance as oil exploration intensified, and Ecuador used part of its oil revenues to buy advanced Israeli Kfir fighter aircraft so as to reduce Peru's military advantage. Renewed Ecuadorean demands for the renegotiation of the Río Protocol in October 1976, and attempts to have the issue raised during negotiations for the Amazon Basin Treaty (July 1978) and in the Andean Pact, inaugurated a further period of tension, marked by armed clashes on their frontier in 1978 and 1981. In the most recent of these, Ecuador claimed that Peru had without provocation attacked three of its military outposts and subjected them to a full-scale bombardment. Peru accused Ecuador of sending military detachments to occupy unused border posts inside Peruvian territory. Five days of fighting in late January 1981 left around 200 dead and the Peruvians claiming total victory. The Ecuadorean reluctance to commit the air force to battle suggests that military concerns may not have been uppermost on this occasion. It is perhaps not a coincidence that the war, which aroused intense nationalist feeling in Ecuador, enabled President Jaime Roldós to rally his flagging supporters and push through controversial price increases which in other circumstances would have surely generated a good deal of domestic opposition and discord. The economic consequences, however, were considerable, as the armed forces were able to demand and get an increase in the military budget, and frightened investors caused a flight of capital as they transferred an estimated three billion *sucres* abroad.

Conflicts with Colombia

Following independence, Ecuador laid claim to the Colombian provinces of Cauca and Pasto, on the basis that these had been part of Ecuador in colonial times. The Ecuadoreans attempted to make good these claims through invasions of Cauca (1830-34) and Pasto (1841-42), but were defeated and expelled by the Colombians. In 1862-63 the two countries fought another brief and inconclusive war. Finally, in 1916, they signed the Muñoz Vernaza-Suarez Treaty settling their frontier disputes, by which Ecuador relinquished her Colombian claims.

Galápagos Islands

US interest in the Galápagos Islands (Archipiélago de Colón) dates from 1854 when Ecuadorean fears of a Peruvian invasion led to the signing of a convention with the US by which, in return for a concession to extract guano there, the US would pay Ecuador three million dollars and provide protection for the archipelago. The subsequent discovery that the Galápagos lacked commercially exploitable deposits of guano left the treaty unfulfilled. In 1910 the government of Eloy Alfaro proposed to lease the islands to the US for 99 years for 15 million dollars. This proposal came to nothing in the face of nationalist opposition in Ecuador which included, in 1911, the first official anti-imperialist platform by a political party, the Conservative Party of Azuay.

On the outbreak of the Second World War, the US became interested in acquiring bases in Latin America and establishing a military presence there. Efforts to persuade Ecuador to grant use of the Galápagos for American military purposes were complicated by the Ecuador-Peru conflict, but in 1942 the islands were made available to the US for the duration of the war. At the same time a small US military base was established at Salinas on the Santa Elena peninsula. In spite of the limited nature of this concession, as early as 1943 some US politicians were advocating that the US should obtain continuing control and use of bases in Latin America after the war, and specifically mentioned the Galápagos as a possibility. In 1944 Washington formally proposed to take a lease on the bases for 99 years, in exchange for giving economic assistance. However, this was rejected by Ecuador and the agreement for the bases expired in 1945. In recent years the importance of the Galápagos as an internationally known scientific and tourism site has given the islands a measure of protection against such ambitions.

Maritime and fishing limits

In common with several Pacific coast countries, Ecuador has claimed a maritime boundary of 200 nautical miles, with exclusive fishing rights inside the zone. This has led to an unresolved conflict with the US, which does not recognise such claims. When President Carlos Julio Arosemena (1961-63) travelled to Washington to negotiate a loan for road construction, approval for it was made conditional on Ecuador releasing US fishing vessels detained within the limit. On his refusal to do this deal, the loan fell through. However, shortly after the overthrow of Arosemena, the miltary government which replaced him (1963-66) signed a secret protocol with the US permitting their vessels to fish within the zone. The dispute returned in the early 1970s when Ecuador and Peru both took a strong line on unauthorised incursions into the exclusive zone, and arrested more than 20 vessels and imposed fines totalling more than one million dollars.

Appendix 2

Velasco Ibarra – the 'stormy petrel' of Ecuadorean politics

The Life and Times

José María Velasco Ibarra was born in Quito in 1893 and educated at the Jesuit college there and at the Central University, from which he graduated as a lawyer and where he briefly lectured in the Faculty of Law. By 1922 he was secretary of the Council of State and in this capacity shared responsibiliy for the brutal suppression of the Guayaquil Workers Confederation demonstrations in November of that year. This was the first major clash between the state and the emergent labour movement, and several hundred demonstrators were killed. His role in this affair did not inhibit him from posing soon afterwards as the authentic spokesman of the poor and oppressed. In 1926 he wrote in his weekly column for the Quito newspaper *El Comercio* (which got him promoted into the Ecuadorean Academy of Language), 'if it weren't for my profound dislike of self-praise, I would call myself frankly, without fear or misgivings, "socialist"'. The main features of his ideological position were already in place by this time – the hostility to organised political parties, the emphasis on moral character, the abuse of elites, the ambivalence of his own political standpoint.

At the beginning of the 1930s he travelled to France and studied at the Sorbonne. He returned to enter Congress for the first time, with clerical backing, in 1932 as deputy for Pichincha; this was the beginning of a political career that was to span almost half a century. In the Congress his talents as an orator and destroyer of governments quickly became manifest, and in 1934, standing as a Liberal but with Conservative support, he was elected President. His political standpoint was characteristically vague and all-embracing. 'My ideology is defined: liberal-individualist ... If socialism has good, worthwhile questions, then we should take them from there. If conservatism can offer us something helpful, we shouldn't refuse it. Nor should the acceptable offerings of communism be excluded.'

His attempt to convert the presidency into a dictatorship in 1935 was not supported by the army and he was overthrown. He stood again in 1939 as a Socialist but lost, in an election widely considered to be fraudulent. After a revolution in 1944 he reached the presidency for the second time, on a platform supposedly promising radical change, but declared himself dictator in 1946, exiled his erstwhile collaborators on the Left and installed a right-wing government. He was shortly afterwards overthrown by his Minister of Defence. He became President for the third time in 1952, standing now as a centrist with support from the conservatives and the right, and succeeded in completing his term of office – the only time he did so. His drift to the right was becoming increasingly apparent by this time. When the railway workers went on strike in June 1955 he warned that '(In this matter) is clearly revealed the the communistoid (sic) revolutionary tendency which is sinisterly and dangerously infiltrating into the administration, into political life, into the national economic base under the protection of a seditious atmosphere created by many capitalist writers.' He was elected for the fourth time in 1960. (His thirst for office led his predecessor, Camilo Ponce, to the observation that, 'we're dealing here with a psychopathic case, since he considers that though he was born like all other human beings, in his case it was wearing the presidential sash'.) He was overthrown a year later by his Vice-President, Arosemena. His fifth and last occupancy of the presidency began in 1968 when he governed with the support of the Liberal Radical Party, his historic enemy, until once again he attempted to convert himself into a dictator and was expelled by the military in 1972. He was frequently in exile, usually in Argentina, his wife's native country, where he lived austerely as a university teacher. He returned to Ecuador in February 1979 to bury his wife, and died there a month later.

At the height of his powers, his style and personality made an extraordinary impact on anyone who heard him speak. 'Tall, spare, quixotesque; with a high forehead which premature baldness progressively enlarged and over which he wore a lumpy felt hat in the town or a straw hat in the countryside; quick bright eyes which glinted behind his spectacles as he jerked his head brusquely to and fro; a moustache like García Moreno's, which turned white early; cheeks as sunken as a fasting hermit; extended neck; the long supple hands of a conjuror, made for hypnotic gestures and the flourishes of thrilling oratory, extended in the air above him, the right index finger shaking in permanent prophetic denunciation; his erect figure standing out from those around him ... elegantly turned out, even in moments of extreme poverty; the dominant speaker in conversation or in debate ... the unmistakeable modulations of his voice, now soothing, now inflaming, crackling with steely nuances, sometimes shrill and strident, with strange inflexions running the whole length of the scale, full of yells, repetitions, outbursts, quivers, reiterated syllables, pauses and above all, taunts and insults – thunderous taunts and insults that leave an indelible impression, pouring out in a tidal wave that sweeps all before it, personal in the extreme ... a style that has had many imitators, though none have succeeded in capturing that same quality of electrifying momentousness. Such is Velasco Ibarra.'

(Jorge Salvador Lara, *Escorzos de historia patria*)

Velasco Ibarra on 'the social problem'

'I don't accept subjective rights nor do I conceive of the human ideal as other than a joint and communal effort by men to increase moral dignity, spiritual understanding and material wellbeing for everyone ... The social problem exists, and in the worst way, because selfishness and ignorance are horrifyingly widespread. Entire villages are unable to grow or satisfy their daily necessities because the *latifundio* owned by a single individual, backed up by an absurd concept of law, surrounds and smothers them; there are workmen who live crammed in hovels without light or space or cleanliness, mothers who don't know what to do with their children because on account of them, they cannot rent a room nor get work to stave off hunger; the Indian, the worker in the fields, lives almost like an animal ... Will there be a true liberal, will there be a true Christian who will be really, truly and positively a socialist?' (1926)

- on the oligarchies in Ecuador

'Undoubted the disorder of the Republic, undeniable the national feebleness. The cause, lack of justice, lack of efficiency, personalist oligarchies. The government has been run for the benefit of particular persons and particular interests; decision and resolution have not been put at the service of the ethical aspirations of the people.' (1934)

- on the Indians

'The Indian in the countryside does not do wrong. He feeds the country with his work. The Indian of the city, in contrast, is supremely dangerous. He has read books.' (1939)

- on politicians and the people

'Those who belong to political groups, who always deny their fundamental political rights to the people, who live only for the hunt for plum jobs and increases in salary, have no right to provoke a phoney and unnecessary communist agitation among a population which needs to produce, to work.' (1926)

'Governments which are not linked to the popular masses fear the surging waves of the multitudes. When government is for the few, the clamour for justice produces situations of instability, distrust and disorder. We must change everything. Let us make of the government an impartial national service. The government should live connected up to, and should clarify, the intuition and sentiments of the people.' (1934)

'The Ecuadorean people, especially those of the coast, belong to no political party.' (1946)

'We must form non parties because the world is not made for parties. We must form movements. Parties are the decayed institutions of the bourgeois stage

104

which has passed. The present moment of this century is the vehement explosion of the demands of the masses, of popular demands, of national demands. We must form groups, movements which get right inside this new hour in which people and nations express themselves and fortify themselves. The worn-out political parties, those anarchic and eccentric groups which appear everywhere today, will never understand this.' (1969)

- on his own character

'My soul is entirely of the left ... For love of the Fatherland, do not ask of me a government of the right or of the left.' (1944)

'I seek nothing for myself. I do not seek comfort or money. I desire to continue being poor to keep my soul revolutionary.' (1945)

- on the ideology and programme of *Velasquismo*

'I can say, without any vain bragging and as a simple fact, that Velasquism is divided into three candidacies: popular revolution, liberal and centre-right. It's difficult for people in other countries to understand this phenomenon. To grasp it it is necessary to have experienced Ecuadorean politics and to know that Velasquism resolved a problem at bottom divisible into various tendencies without losing its unifying essence.' (1955)

'This is what Velasquism is: a liberal doctrine, a Christian doctrine, a socialist doctrine.' (1960)

- on moral regeneration

'They call you the despicable rabble because you are *Velasquistas* ... This rabble is the soul of the Fatherland, this is the rabble that will redeem the Republic from the corruption, from the selfish, calculating and corrupt stagnation in which it lies today. Yes! This is the rabble that will purify us, will give us strength and raise us up.' (1960)

- on the art of government

'The present moment is not of the Right nor of the Left. It is a synthesis of energies to reconstruct a Fatherland in agony. I am a man of the Left, but I accept the nature of things and as a leader I place myself in the centre ... They have done me the very great honour of converting me into a point of convergence and harmony ... The art of government cannot be learned in books. One of the grave defects in our leaders has been ... to become excessively enthusiastic about sonorous programmes of government. The government is always directed by the nature of things, as Napoleon wisely said.' (1944)

Appendix 3

The CIA in Ecuador in the 1960s

'We aren't running the country but we are certainly helping to shape events'

The early 1960s were good times for the US Central Intelligence Agency. The Washington foreign policy establishment was in a state of near-hysteria about the 'communist threat' posed by Fidel Castro and the revolution in Cuba, President Kennedy (whose favourite reading was Ian Fleming's James Bond novels) was an enthusiast for covert operations, and American public opinion had not yet been disillusioned by the Vietnam War and Nixon about the excesses committed in its name by its government's secret agencies.

Against this background, the CIA had a virtually free hand in Latin America. One of 'the Company's' agents, Philip Agee, served in Ecuador in 1960-63 and subsequently in Uruguay, but later became disillusioned about the role and actions of the CIA and resigned in 1968. Soon afterwards he published a diary of his experiences as an operative. The following extracts – a rare chink of light into the murky world of international espionage – illustrate the way that the CIA tried systematically to subvert and corrupt the government and administration of a friendly country.

'[Dr Felipe Ovalle] has a modest medical practice, most of which comes from his inclusion on the US Embassy list of approved medical examiners for Ecuadorean applicants for visas. [His] agent file reveals that verification of his medical degree, supposedly obtained at a Colombian university, has proved impossible. Through the years he has developed a close relationship with President Velasco, whom he now serves as a personal physician. Ovalle reports the results of his weekly meetings with Velasco to the station.'

'[Colonel Wilfredo Oswaldo Lugo, Chief of Personnel of National Police Headquarters] is considered to be a penetration of the security service and in times of crisis his reporting is invaluable, since he is in a position to give situation reports on government plans and reactions to events as reflected in orders to police and military units ... Noland [chief of the CIA Quito Station] also pays a regular monthly salary to Colonel Lugo.'

'[Lt. Colonel Roger Paredes] runs a five-man full-time team for surveillance and general investigations in Quito ... Another sub-agent is the chief of the identity card section of the Ministry of Government. As all citizens are required to register and obtain an official government-issued identity card, this agent provides on request the full name, date and place of birth, names of parents, occupation, address and photograph of practically any Ecuadorean.'

'Recruitment of Varea [Lt Colonel Reinaldo Varea Donoso, a retired army officer], an important leader of Velasquistas in military circles, proceeded with the assistance of Kladensky. Funds were provided by Noland ... for Varea's successful campaign for the Senate, and in August he was elected Vice-President of the Senate. He reports on military support for Velasco and he maintains regular contact with the leadership in the Ministry of Defense and the principal military units. Varea's station salary of $700 per month is high by Ecuadorean standards but his access to crucial intelligence on government policy and stability is adequate justification. The project also provides funds for a room rented full-time in Ladensky's name in the new, luxurious Hotel Quito where Kadensky and Varea take their playmates.'

'The major station agent for placing propaganda is Gustavo Salgado, an ex-communist considered by many to be the outstanding liberal political journalist in the country. His column appears several times per week in *El Comercio*, the main Quito daily, and in several provincial newspapers ... Proper treatment of Ecuadorean and international themes is worked out in the station by John Bacon ... and passed to the agent for final draft.'

'The most important station operation for anti-communist political action consists of funding and guidance to selected leaders of the Conservative Party and the Social Christian Movement. The operation developed from the most important station penetration of the Ponce government, Renato Pérez Drouet, who was Secretary General of Administration under Ponce ... [Aurelio Dávila Cajas] is now the fastest rising young leader in the Conservative Party and very closely associated with the Catholic Church hierarchy which the party represents in politics ... The station is now helping him to build up his personal political organisation.'

'The propaganda and political-action campaign against Araujo [Manuel Araujo, leftist politician, briefly Minister of Government in Velasco's fourth administration], Cuba and communism in general has clearly been the major station programme since I arrived six months ago. The [code-name ECACTOR] project has accounted for much of this activity. It costs about $50,000 a year and in a place like Quito a thousand dollars a week buys a lot. The feelings I have is that we aren't running the country but we are certainly helping to shape events in the direction and form we want.'

'The first new operation is with Carlos Roggiero, a retired Army captain and one of the principal Social Christian representatives on the National Defense

107

Front. Roggiero is chief of the Social Christian militant-action squads, including the secret bomb-squad, and I have started training him in the use of various incendiary, crowd dispersement and harassment devices that I requested from [Technical Services Division] in headquarters. Through him we will form perhaps ten squads, of five to ten men each, for disrupting meetings and small demonstrations and for general street control and intimidation...'

'[Following the seizure of power by the military in July 1963] Gandara [Colonel Marcos Gandara, leader of the junta] has given approval in principle to a joint telephone-tapping operation in which we will provide the equipment and the transcribers and he will arrange the connections in the telephone exchange and provide cover ... After this operation gets going we'll save Rafael Bucheli for monitoring sensitive political lines without the knowledge of the Junta ... Right now there are about 125 political prisoners in Quito, including not only communists but Velasquistas and members of the Concentration of Popular Forces. The Junta policy is to allow them to go into exile, although some will be able to stay in Ecuador depending on their political antecedents – judgement of which, in most cases, is based on information we're passing to Colonel Luis Mora Bowen, the Minister of Government.'

'Ricardo Vázquez Díaz, one of the labour agents I took over from Gil Saudade, told me the other day that his mistress is the official shorthand transcriber of all the important meetings of the Cabinet and the Junta and that she has been giving him copies so that he can be well-informed for his [trade union] work. He gave me samples and after Dean saw them he told me to start paying her a salary through Vázquez. From now on we'll be getting copies of the record of these meetings even before the participants ... These reports are jewels of political intelligence – just the sort of intelligence that covert action operations should produce.'

'The Minister of Government is very cooperative in following our advice over the matter of the political prisoners. We have a special interrogation team here now from the US Army Special Forces unit in the Canal Zone: they're from the counter-guerrilla school there and are helping process the interrogation reports and prepare follow-up leads.'

Philip Agee *Inside the Company: CIA Diary*, 1975

Appendix 4

The Assault on the Amazon

One of the consequences of the Febres government's 'open door' economic model has been to encourage multinational capital to exploit the resources of the Amazon in Ecuador's *Oriente* region. This has accelerated a process which was already under way and which threatens to unleash an environmental and human catastrophe. Hitherto small-scale and limited frontier expansion into eastern Ecuador was strongly boosted by the discovery of oil towards the end of the 1960s and the rapid construction by Texaco and other transnational companies of roads, pipelines and new towns to service their exploitation of the region's wealth. Among the most active and useful agents of the multinationals' penetration of the new lands have been US Protestant evangelical groups, who have taken on the task of 'pacifying' and 'civilising' the Indians on their behalf, and even directly prospecting for oil.

Prominent among these groups has been the Summer Institute for Linguistics (SIL), founded in 1942 by William Campbell Townsend as a vehicle for evangelising among the Cackchiquel Indians of Guatemala. Connected to the Wycliffe Bible Translators, the SIL presents itself as a respectable scientific organisation, whose aim is to encourage Spanish literacy among Indian communities in Latin America. Critics of the SIL allege, however, that the organisation works in cooperation with regional governments to destroy Indian cultural identity and, where necessary, to disrupt and transplant communities.

The SIL arrived in Ecuador in 1952 and signed contracts for bilingual, health and occupational training programmes. From 1968 to 1972, the group cooperated with the government and oil companies to remove the Huaorani and Auca Indians from oil lands to reservations. Land pressure among *mestizo* peasants in the Andean *sierra* led the government to encourage settlement along the roads to the jungle oil wells and Africa palm plantations, and the removal of Indians was an essential precondition of this policy. The SIL was also directly involved in prospecting. At one time, for instance, the organisation was reported to have more geologists and scientists attached to its team than it had language specialists. A presidential decree of 1981, banning SIL activity in Ecuador, was the result of pressure from Indian organisations. Experience in Peru and Colombia indicates, however, that the aggressively fundamentalist SIL is a resilient body.

The rush to extract the 'black gold' has inflicted severe damage on the rain forests. Oil spillages have polluted rivers and vast tracts of forest have been cut down to make way for the companies' installations. Land-hungry colonists have come in the wake of the big foreign corporations, and the indigenous population, with their traditional lands and resources under threat from the intruders, have begun a desperate struggle for survival.

Estimates put the number of indigenous people in the *Oriente* at around 70,000. Five Indian groups (Quichua, Huaorani, Cofan, Siona and Secoya) have already been heavily affected, and new oil exploration contracts are taking the problem into territory occupied by the Shuar and Achuar Indians. These peoples do not enjoy official government protection. In fact Ecuador has never formulated a specific policy for the protection of the Amazonian tribes. In their efforts to promote national integration and economic development, successive governments have ignored ethnic differences and urged assimilation. The insensitivity of this approach is exemplified by Rodríguez Lara who in 1972 claimed that 'There is no more Indian problem. We all become white men when we accept the goals of the national culture'.

Historically, the policies of the state towards the *Oriente* have been shaped by three basic concerns: to ease the land shortage elsewhere in the country by encouraging colonisation eastwards; to exploit the region's potentially great natural resources; and to prevent a further loss of national territory. The demand for land, especially in the highlands, was a permanent source of social and economic discontent; to have brought about a large-scale redistribution would have needed a revolution. The 1964 and 1973 agrarian reform laws proposed to use the *Oriente* as an escape valve for these pressures by promoting colonisation of *tierras baldías* (uncultivated lands). Government agencies (IERAC, CREA and INCREA) have actively favoured the white and *mestizo* settlers and paid only lip-service to the rights and interests of the Indians. When concern about ethnic and ecological issues has been expressed, it has been overridden by powerful economic and political interests which have the ear of the Ministry of Agriculture in Quito. Although land titles have been granted to Indians, they are often ignored by the oil companies, and in some areas 'conservation zones' have been deliberately created by the government, not to protect the Indians but to keep settlers out and enable oil extraction to take place without hindrance. There has been little recognition or understanding of the Indians' own ethnic traditions or of the land-use requirements for hunting, fishing and food-gathering.

The tragic qualities of such policies were dramatically illustrated in July 1987, when a Catholic bishop, Alejandro Labaca, and the nun who was accompanying him, Sister Inés Arango, tried to make contact with a group of Huaorani Indians called the Red Feet. In a gruesome ritual, the Indians pinned the missionaries to the forest floor with 21 spears, each 12 feet long and decorated with rope ornaments. The bodies when found also bore 109 other

110

spear wounds, many of which had been stuffed with leaves to staunch the flow of blood and prolong the victims' agony. Beside them, the Indians had erected a pole with a bone tied to it, as a warning to other intruders into their territory. This is not the first time the Huaoranis have reacted with violence to uninvited intrusions. The first whites to contact them in 1956, a group of fundamentalist missionaries from the US, were also speared to death, and since 1977 there have been at least a dozen fatal attacks by Huaorani on workers of the oil, timber and palm oil companies. But as the stakes in the Ecuadorean Amazon rise ever higher, the likelihood of reprisals by the Ecuadorean army increases, and the very survival of the Red Feet is now in question. However, in February 1988 a treaty co-signed by the government and the Ecuadorean bishops' conference ruled that 100,000 acres of ancestral Huaorani land should be off limits for petroleum exploration companies. Whether the government is willing or able to enforce this remains to be seen.

Economic development has always had priority over Indian protection and recent governments have given contracts on generous terms to foreign and national companies to explore for minerals such as gold and uranium and to exploit the *Oriente's* timber stands. The government's past indifference to the plight of the indigenous inhabitants is also explained by the region's strategic importance. In its efforts to protect the oil installations and further its territorial claims in the Amazon, Quito has been unwilling to accept that Indian cultural areas do not coincide with disputed international frontiers. Consequently, the Secoya Indians, whose traditional homelands extend into both Colombian and Peruvian territory, are often persecuted as spies because they cross into territory controlled by the latter country. Sionas and Secoya frequently complain of harsh treatment at the hands of the Ecuadorean army, including forced labour, involuntary conscription and rape.

The Indian struggle to hold on to their remaining lands is facing a new challenge in the 1980s. African palm plantations have long been established west of the Andes but are now spreading into Amazonia, bringing new forms of exploitation and ethnocide to the areas around the Shushufindi and Huashito rivers where the Secoya, Siona and Quichua peoples have their home. In March 1984 a Central Bank report declared that 400,000 hectares were immediately available for a palm oil agro-industrial project and a further 250,000 hectares were suitable for planting. Encouraged by the government, which sees palm oil as a major export earners, foreign capital has been attracted by the high yields obtainable in the *Oriente*. Colombian credits are enabling *Palmeras del Ecuador* to build a processing plant and expand its plantations to 5,000 hectares, with further plans for expansion to 100,000 hectares. Another company, *Palmoriente SA*, which plans a 40 million dollar palm oil investment, derives 40 per cent of its capital from European sources (19 per cent from SCSS of Belgium, 15 per cent from Britain's Commonwealth Development Corporation and six per cent from the West German Development Corporation, along with technical assistance from a French research institute).

The existing palm oil plantations have already taken their toll of the environment. Insecticides and toxic waste emitted during processing have

111

polluted the rivers around them and led to the wholesale destruction of large areas of tropical forest. This latest invasion poses a potentially greater threat to the indigenous population than previous waves of missionaries, oil companies and colonists into the area. Apart from destroying the forest resources upon which the Indians depend for food and shelter, canoes and agricultural implements, these new developments seem likely to force the Indians into becoming cheap wage-labour for plantations and agro-industries. Once reduced to the condition of poorly-paid labourers and with their natural habitat destroyed, the Indians' own culture seems bound to suffer and perhaps disappear for ever.

However, there are oases of hope in this gloomy scene, as the Río Mazán project, 20 kilometres from Cuenca, testifies. The ecologically rich mountain forest region of southern Ecuador came under threat in 1976 from a plan to export timber to the US for furniture making. Following a campaign by *Fundación Natura*, Ecuador's conservation organisation, tree-felling was halted and the area was acquired by the people of Cuenca, who in 1984 raised 33,000 dollars to buy it. By doing so, they were able to launch Ecuador's first-ever conservation initiative and turn Mazán into a nature reserve and 'people's forest'. More recently, *Fundación Natura* has successfully campaigned to have restrictions on the importation of dangerous pesticides reimposed after the government had removed them. The richness and importance of Ecuador's ecological endowment is illustrated by the fact that there have been estimated to be more than 20,000 different species of plants in the country, compared with only 17,000 plant species in the whole of the US.

Further Reading

The following brief list concentrates mainly on books in English published in the last ten years. Most have a good bibliography of works in Spanish, articles and earlier books.

Nelson Argones, *El juego del poder*, Quito, CEN, 1985

George Blanksten, *Ecuador: Constitutions and Caudillos*, New York, Russell & Russell, 1964

R J Bromley, *Development Planning in Ecuador*, London, Latin American Publications Fund, 1977

Agustín Cueva, *The Process of Political Domination in Ecuador*, New Brunswick, Transaction Books, 1982

J S Fitch, *The Military Coup d'Etat as a Political Process, Ecuador 1948-1966*, Baltimore, Johns Hopkins University Press, 1977

Charles R Gibson, *Foreign Trade in the Economic Development of Small Nations: The Case of Ecuador*, New York, Praeger, 1971

Osvaldo Hurtado, *Political Power in Ecuador*, Albuquerque, University of New Mexico Press, 1980

John D Martz, *Ecuador: Conflicting Political Culture and the Quest for Progress*, Boston, Allyn & Bacon, 1972

Nick D Mills, *Crisis, conflicto y consenso: Ecuador 1979-1984*, Quito, Cordes, 1984

Frederick B Pike, *The United States and the Andean Republics: Peru, Bolivia and Ecuador*, Cambridge, Mass., Harvard University Press, 1977

Michael Redclift, *Agrarian Reform and Peasant Organizations on the Ecuadorean Coast*, London, Athlone Press, 1978

Linda A Rodríguez, *The Search for Public Policy, Regional Politics and Government Finances in Ecuador 1830-1940*, Berkeley, University of California Press, 1985

Augusto Varas and Fernando Bustamente, *Fuerzas armadas y política en Ecuador*, Quito, Ediciones Latinoamerica, 1978

David H Zook, Jnr., *Zarumilla-Marañon: The Ecuador-Peru Dispute*, New York, Bookman Associates, 1964

New LAB books

The Great Tin Crash: Bolivia and the World Tin Market
Tells the story of tin; from the rise of the tin can to the collapse of the world tin market in October 1985, and its impact on the mineworkers and their families in Bolivia.
'We recommend it to be read by all mineworkers unions.' Miners International Federation.
Price £3.70

Green Gold: Bananas and Dependency in the Eastern Caribbean
Looks at the history, recent developments and future prospects for the banana industry in Dominica, Grenada, St Lucia and St Vincent, focusing on conditions for the region's small farmers.
Price £4.70

Guatemala: False Hope, False Freedom
Draws upon recent research in Guatemala by the author, James Painter, to examine the enduring chasm between the rich and the poor, the continued counter-insurgency campaign, and the policies of President Cerezo's Christian Democrat party.
Published jointly with the Catholic Institute for International Relations.
Price £5.50

Soft Drink, Hard Labour: Guatemalan Workers Take on Coca-Cola
Miguel Angel Reyes and Mike Gatehouse
Covers the recent history of the struggle of the Coca-Cola workers in Guatemala against their management, including the 1984 occupation, the general political and trade union context behind it, and Coca-Cola's local and international response to it.
Price £1.50

The Thatcher Years: Britain and Latin America
Analyses the politics of aid, trade and debt; assesses British policy towards dictatorships and democracies in Chile and Argentina; and reveals Britain's support for US action in Central America and the Caribbean.
Price £3.50

Prices include post and packing
For a complete list of LAB books write to LAB, 1 Amwell Street, London EC1R 1UL.

LAB is a small, independent, non-profit-making research organisation established in 1977. LAB is concerned with human rights and related social, political and economic issues in Central and South America and the Caribbean. We carry out research and publish books, publicise and lobby on these issues and establish support links with Latin American groups. We also brief the media, organise seminars and have a growing programme of schools publications.